CULTURES OF THE WORLD

Singapore

mc **Marshall Cavendish**
Benchmark
New York

PICTURE CREDITS

Cover: © Robert Harding Picture Library/SuperStock
Alain Evrard/Robert Harding/Getty Images: 92 • Aun Koh/Lonely Planet Images: 126, 131 • Chew Seng Kim/
The Straits Times/Getty Images: 6 • Felix Hug/Lonely Planet Images: 73, 95• Glenn Beanland/Lonely Planet
Images: 10 • Holger Leue/Lonely Planet Images: 7 • Inmagine: 1, 11, 15, 16, 19, 31, 34, 45, 47, 52, 56, 66, 69,
70, 79, 80, 82, 88, 93, 100, 101, 102, 104, 106, 109, 118, 125, 130 • Kevin Clogstoun/Lonely Planet Images: 84, 90
Mark Daffey/Lonely Planet Images: 63 • Marshall Cavendish International (Asia): 135 • Michael Coyne/Lonely
Planet Images: 74 • Munshi Ahmed/Bloomberg/Getty Images: 30 • Northwind Picture Archives: 22 • Paul
Kennedy/Lonely Planet Images: 54, 57, 78 • Paul Popper/Popperfoto/Getty Images: 23 • Phil Weymouth/Lonely
Planet Images: 44, 53, 87 • Philip Game/Lonely Planet Images: 55 • Photolibrary: 3, 9, 13, 14, 18, 26, 35, 36,
48, 98 • Richard I'Anson/Lonely Planet Images: 46, 94 • Roslan Rahman/AFP/Getty Images: 29, 37, 39, 42, 50,
64, 67, 68, 72 • Shirlyn Loo/Flickr/Getty Images: 60 • Simin Wang/AFP/Getty Images: 97 • Simon Richmond/
Lonely Planet Images: 76 • Singapore Tourism Board: 8, 108, 110, 113, 115, 120, 122 • Tom Cockrem/Lonely
Planet Images: 5, 86, 127 • Tomohiro Ohsumi/Bloomberg/Getty Images: 32 • Toshifumi Kitamura/AFP/Getty
Images: 27 • Toshiyuki Aizawa/Bloomberg/Getty Images: 28 • Wayne Eastep/Getty Images: 38 • Wendy Chan/
The Image Bank/Getty Images: 41

PRECEDING PAGE

Malay students waving the Singapore flag in the Geylang Serai District.

Publisher (U.S.): Michelle Bisson
Writers: Lesley Layton, Pang Guek Cheng, and Jo-Ann Kee-Spilling
Editors: Deborah Grahame-Smith, Stephanie Pee
Copyreader: Sherry Chiger
Designers: Nancy Sabato, Benson Tan
Cover picture researcher: Tracey Engel
Picture researcher: Joshua Ang

Marshall Cavendish Benchmark
99 White Plains Road
Tarrytown, NY 10591
Website: www.marshallcavendish.us

Originated and designed by Times Media Private Limited
An imprint of Marshall Cavendish International (Asia) Private Limited
A member of Times Publishing Limited

Marshall Cavendish is a trademark of Times Publishing Limited.

Library of Congress Cataloging-in-Publication Data
Layton, Lesley, 1954-
  Singapore / Lesley Layton, Pang Guek Cheng, Jo-Ann Spilling. — 3rd ed.
    p. cm. — (Cultures of the world)
  Includes bibliographical references and index.
  Summary: "Provides comprehensive information on the geography, history, wildlife, governmental structure,
economy, cultural diversity, peoples, religion, and culture of Singapore"—Provided by publisher.
  ISBN 978-1-60870-787-4 (print)
  1. Singapore—Juvenile literature. I. Pang, Guek-Cheng, 1950- II. Spilling, Jo-Ann. III. Title. IV. Series.

DS609.L38 2012
959.57—dc22   2011004479

Printed in Malaysia
7 6 5 4 3 2 1

CONTENTS

SINGAPORE TODAY   **5**

1. GEOGRAPHY
Topography • Rivers • The city • Climate • Flora and fauna   **11**

2. HISTORY
Early history • Political history • Social history   **19**

3. GOVERNMENT
National government • Local authorities • Legal structures   **27**

4. ECONOMY
Industries • Cottage industries • Sources of revenue • Work ethic   **35**

5. ENVIRONMENT
Green lungs • The air we breathe • Every drop counts • Health and food hygiene   **45**

6. SINGAPOREANS
Main ethnic groups • The Singaporean identity • Names • Costume   **53**

7. LIFESTYLE
Social interaction • Family • Children • Women • Birth • Puberty • Marriage and divorce • Death   **63**

8. RELIGION
Main religions • Places of worship • Holy symbols • Folk beliefs   **79**

9. LANGUAGE
A diversity of tongues • Nonverbal language • Script   **87**

10. ARTS Theater and drama • Dance • Music • Art and artifacts • Literature **93**

11. LEISURE Games • Sports • Storytelling • Vacation pursuits • Hobbies and pastimes **101**

12. FESTIVALS Taoist/Buddhist festivals • Muslim festivals • Hindu festivals • Christian festivals • Nonreligious celebrations **109**

13. FOOD Main ethnic groups and their cuisines • Foods and their sources • Kitchens • Eating habits • Eating out • Food taboos • Food beliefs • Table manners • Feasts **119**

MAP OF SINGAPORE **132**

ABOUT THE ECONOMY **135**

ABOUT THE CULTURE **137**

TIME LINE **138**

GLOSSARY **140**

FOR FURTHER INFORMATION **141**

BIBLIOGRAPHY **142**

INDEX **143**

SINGAPORE TODAY

SINGAPORE, A TINY ISLAND ONE DEGREE NORTH OF THE EQUATOR, lies at the tip of the Asian mainland, just south of Thailand and Malaysia. This strategic position, together with a natural harbor, enabled the 19th-century fishing village to flourish into the modern city it is today. It did this through the hard work of the indigenous people and migrants from China, India, and Europe who were attracted by the opportunity to make a good life in the bustling port. Their descendants made the island one of the busiest and most successful ports in the world, as well as an important financial center for Southeast Asia.

Migration continues to be an important element in the success of Singapore even today as it opens its doors to people from all over the world. After all, its citizens are Singapore's greatest resource. Their resilience and ability to adapt to a fast-changing and technologically driven world continues to be the key to Singapore's economic success. Today Singapore's population of almost 5.1 million includes citizens of Malay, Chinese, and Indian descent as well as many thousands of permanent residents and foreign workers from across Southeast and South Asia.

A group of Singaporean National Servicemen on a military exercise.

To grow its population, Singapore has granted permanent residency (PR) status to many noncitizens who are working and living in the republic although they were born in other countries. Their PR status entitles them to most of the rights and duties of citizens, including eligibility for public housing and mandatory National Service for young adult males. However, permanent residents do not have the right to vote in general elections. Between 1990 and 2000, the number of permanent residents increased by approximately 10 percent annually, outstripping the number of Singaporean citizens, which grew by just more than 1 percent annually. The majority of permanent residents come from the neighboring countries of Malaysia, China (including Hong Kong), and Taiwan.

Known as a clean and efficient city, Singapore is unique in many ways. In both its politics and its economics, it manages to blend democracy and capitalism with some government intervention. In its architecture, Singapore's glass-and-steel skyscrapers comfortably sit alongside its historic shop houses and ancient temples. Singapore also manages to embrace modernity while maintaining many of its traditions. Singapore's diverse

A view of Singapore's skyline. Despite its small size, Singapore has one of the most stable economies in Southeast Asia.

population lives together harmoniously in spite of its different religions and languages.

Although Singapore is lacking in natural resources and space, it has managed to build and maintain a strong and successful economy that is one of the most highly developed in the region. When Singapore abruptly gained independence in 1965, it was poor and struggling with bleak prospects. Against the odds, the republic has grown into one of Asia's "dragon economies," joining the ranks of the richest countries in the world.

Many cultures and peoples have influenced the history of Singapore. From the 14th to the 16th centuries, the island was ruled by the Siamese, the Javanese, and the sultans of both Malacca and Johor. Later, during the 17th and 18th centuries, the Portuguese and the British controlled the island. The British ruled from 1867 until independence in 1965, except during part of World War II, when the Japanese ruled Singapore from 1942 to 1945. Even today in modern Singapore, there are strong reminders of British rule.

The most notable remnant of British rule is that English is widely spoken throughout the republic. English is taught at schools and is the language of business. The educated middle classes speak English at home and at work. The lower classes, however, tend to speak English at work and to communicate in their own ethnic dialects while at home or among friends. Singapore has its own version of English—dubbed Singlish—which is a blend of British English and Malay, Chinese, and Indian words and inflections.

Life in modern Singapore is highly urbanized and can be hectic. Space is at a premium, and a large proportion of the population live in affordable but compact high-rise government-subsidized apartments. Many Singaporeans aspire to move out of these apartments into their own privately owned luxury condominiums. A small percentage of the population is wealthy enough to own houses. In spite of space constraints, the standard of living is high, although many Singaporeans complain that the cost of living is just as high. Generally Singaporeans enjoy a good lifestyle and have easy access to an excellent health care and education system as well as a reliable communications and transportation infrastructure.

The Mass Rapid Transit train system is part of Singapore's highly efficient public transportation system.

Work is a dominant feature in the lives of many Singaporeans. People work hard at their jobs and put in long hours; it is not unusual to work six days a week. Children are expected to work hard at school from a very young age. Many Singaporeans aspire to attain both professional and material success, and as a result, living and working in Singapore can be stressful at times.

The main pastime among Singaporeans, both young and old, is shopping. The city is a shoppers' paradise, and there are large departmental stores as well as smaller specialty shops everywhere. Shops are open for long hours, from as early as 9 A.M. to as late as 10 P.M. Shopping malls are always crowded with people who gather to socialize after school or after work.

Singapore is described by many as a food paradise. In fact eating is a favorite pastime of most Singaporeans.

Eating is another favorite pastime among Singaporeans. There is an enormous range of cuisines from all over the world. When it comes to food, Singaporeans are spoiled for choice. Food is served in expensive gourmet restaurants as well as in affordable food courts. As it is possible to eat out relatively cheaply, many busy Singaporean families often have their meals in local restaurants or hawker centers (outdoor food courts) in their neighborhood or buy food to take home for dinner most weekdays. The tropical climate allows Singaporeans to enjoy the outdoors regularly. Swimming, sailing, and bicycling are popular hobbies. Singaporeans also enjoy the cinema and simply meeting up with friends and family for a chat in a café or coffee shop.

Singapore today is almost unrecognizable from the period just after it gained independence in 1965. In less than 50 years, this tiny island with no natural resources has managed to miraculously transform itself into an impressive modern city with a promising future.

GEOGRAPHY

A view of the city of Singapore. With a population of over 5 million people, most of the island is densely built up.

THE REPUBLIC OF SINGAPORE lies at the southern tip of Peninsular Malaysia. In addition to the main island of Singapore, there are more than 60 offshore islets. Settlements of wood-and-zinc huts on stilts are still to be found on some of these islets, but the residents have gradually relocated to the main island.

Other islets play an important economic role, as locations for oil refineries or pleasure resorts. Among the islets, the larger ones include Pulau Tekong, Pulau Ubin, and Sentosa.

Rain over one of Singapore's islands, Pulau Ubin.

THE REPUBLIC OF SINGAPORE

Singapore is 85 miles (137 km) north of the equator, making it the Asian city nearest to the equator. The main island of Singapore is about 26 miles (42 km) from east to west and 14 miles (23 km) from north to south. It is about 3.5 times the size of Washington D.C.

The island's coastline of about 120 miles (193 km) encloses a land area of 238 square miles (616 square km). Including the offshore islets, Singapore's total area is 269 square miles (697 square km) and growing: Land is constantly being reclaimed from the sea, and it is estimated that land area will increase by about another 39 square miles (100 square km) by the year 2030. The highest point is the Bukit Timah Nature Reserve, which is 538 feet (164 m) above sea level.

TOPOGRAPHY

"It is impossible to conceive a place combining more advantages; it is within a week's sail of China, still closer to Siam, Cochin-China, in the very heart of the Archipelago, or as the Malays call it, 'the Navel of the Malay countries.'"
—Sir Stamford Raffles, founder of modern Singapore

The main island of Singapore consists of three regions: highlands in the center, a gently undulating area in the west, and a flat eastern region. Singapore was originally covered with tropical rain forests and the coasts fringed with mangrove swamps, but all these have since been altered. The city lies mainly in the south, and the parks, gardens, and agricultural land in the north.

RIVERS

Despite its unimpressive size, the Singapore River has always been the center of any settlement on the island because of its vital role in trade, the country's lifeblood. The river, which is only 1.9 miles (3 km) long, flows into a wide natural harbor whose calm waters allow undisturbed anchorage for small vessels.

In the past, trading boats crammed the harbor, but tidal changes made it unsuitable for large ships. So when steamships were introduced, they moved to the deep narrow waterway between the main island and Sentosa, the largest of the offshore islands, and small barges and bumboats plied the river to bring goods inland.

Once the center of noisy activity, the river has since been cleaned and cleared of traffic. The warehouses that once stored cargo along its edges have been converted for other uses. The quay is being livened up by landscaping, and pleasure cruises upriver have been introduced.

Other rivers, such as the Kallang and its tributaries, act as catchment areas over which dams have been built to create artificial lakes that store rainwater. The oldest and largest reservoirs are located on high ground in the center of the island to catch the heaviest rainfall, while newer reservoirs along the west coast provide water to homes and factories sprouting up on that part of the island.

There are now 14 reservoirs and not enough land to accommodate more, so water is carefully conserved. Much of it must be bought from the state of Johor, in the south of Malaysia, to meet the demands of Singapore's expanding population. Unlike that of many other Asian countries, Singapore's water is chemically treated, so it is safe to drink straight from the tap.

The Singapore River along Clarke Quay.

THE CITY

Over the years the focal point of the city has shifted inland from the shoreline and has become the Central Business District, an area of high-rise offices, banks, stores, and restaurants. The city center now lies behind this, among hotels and department stores. Scattered around the city are the industrial areas and a series of small satellite towns, each with its own services and facilities.

Singapore prides itself on the "greening" program that has earned it the nickname of Garden City. The government makes great efforts to build "green lungs" of parks and gardens throughout the urban districts, planting thousands of ornamental shrubs and trees to keep pace with the city's rapid growth and soften the monotony of concrete.

A network of roads and expressways crisscross the country. To lessen traffic problems in the inner-city areas, the Mass Rapid Transit (MRT) system was introduced. Construction began in 1983, and by 1990 the MRT system was fully operational. Tracks and stations have been built above and below ground to connect the main housing areas with the city, allowing people to travel more comfortably and more quickly.

Despite being heavily built up, the Singapore government has tried to include as much nature and greenery into the city as possible.

CLIMATE

The average daily temperature is 81°F (27°C), varying little more than a few degrees throughout the year. Singapore can be extremely humid, with the average annual relative humidity at more than 80 percent. This hot, humid climate is due to the island's proximity to the equator and to its exposure to a sea lacking cold currents.

Unlike countries in the temperate zone, Singapore has no distinct seasons. The country lies in the path of two monsoons, causing rainfall all year round, but especially during the northeast monsoon, from December to March. From June to September, during the southwest monsoon, much of the rain falls in short showers interspersed with sunshine. In the months between monsoons, thunderstorms are common. Singapore receives an average of 90 inches (229 cm) of rainfall per year, or 7.5 inches (19 cm) per month. The driest months are usually March and April, while November and December are the wettest. In 2010, the month of February was reported to be the driest month in Singapore since 1869, when only 0.25 inches (6.3 millimeters) of rain fell.

FLORA AND FAUNA

Singapore's warm, moist conditions give rise to lush natural vegetation that once covered the entire island. Much of this growth was cleared long ago

Singapore experiences rainfall all year round.

A Malayan monitor lizard at the Sungei Buloh Wetland Reserve in Singapore.

for marine fish farming and timber products, leaving little swamp and meager patches of primary, secondary, and mangrove growth still on the island.

Modernization and land reclamation have been responsible for the loss of many wildlife species, but for its size, Singapore still has one of the most varied ecological habitats in the world. A few stretches of seashore undisturbed by reclamation or development support reef coral, crabs, and various kinds of seaweed. The Singaporean species of freshwater crab is found nowhere else in the world.

Native plants are dwindling fast; most of Singapore's plants are imported species introduced mainly for shade and color. In its early years, the Singapore Botanic Gardens played an important role in fostering agricultural development in the region through collecting, growing, and distributing important plants, including—beginning in 1877—the rubber plant from Ceylon.

In the Bukit Timah Nature Reserve, it is still possible to see the limited areas of primary rain forest left in Singapore. The Bukit Timah Nature Reserve is home to an abundance of indigenous plants. It is also home to numerous small mammals, including the civet cat, the flying lemur, and the tree shrew. Creatures such as the leaf monkey, the mouse-deer, and the wild boar died out long ago with the loss of their natural habitat. The tiger disappeared when the last one was shot in 1932.

An expanse of swampland has been turned into a large bird sanctuary, as Singapore is a haven for migrant birds from September to April each year. Some of the birds, such as the Chinese egret, are endangered species.

Reptiles ranging from the house gecko to the water monitor are common. There are 40 types of snakes, but only a few, such as the cobra and the coral snake, are poisonous.

THE HOUSE GECKO

The island's best-known member of the lizard family is the harmless house gecko. Its feet are equipped with tiny hairs and claws, allowing it to run upside down along ceilings. It is one of the few wild creatures that can live harmoniously with people. Houses shelter it from outside predators, and in return the lizard consumes most of the insects attracted indoors by electric lights.

House geckos easily lose their tails. This is a ploy because the twitching of a shed tail usually startles an enemy long enough for the lizard to make its escape. A new tail always grows, but a series of bumps and ridges gives away the number of tails lost. The Malay name for the gecko is cicak *(chee-chak), after the sound it makes. This loud clicking is familiar in Singapore homes, as are the gecko's fragile white eggs nestling behind bookcases and picture frames.*

INTERNET LINKS

www.asianinfo.org/asianinfo/singapore/pro-geography.htm

This website offers a comprehensive overview about the geography and climate of Singapore.

www.guidemesingapore.com/relocation/introduction/climate-in-singapore

This site is intended for people who intend to relocate to Singapore and covers a wide range of topics ranging from climate to history, to help others understand a bit more about the country.

http://mangrove.nus.edu.sg/guidebooks/contents.htm

An interesting look at the mangrove systems in Singapore.

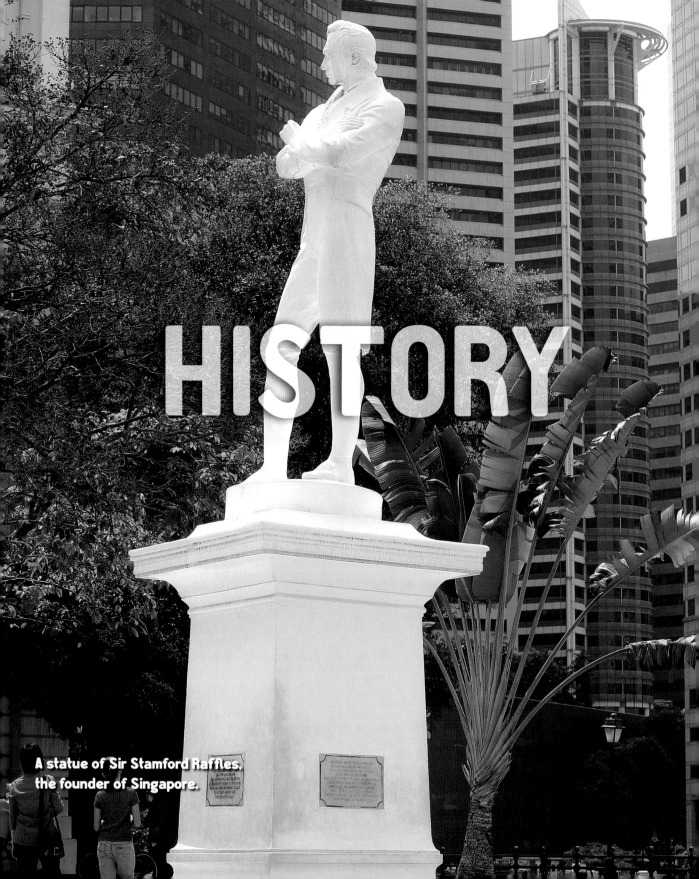

HISTORY

A statue of Sir Stamford Raffles, the founder of Singapore.

2

LITTLE IS KNOWN ABOUT ANCIENT Singapore. One of the earliest references to Singapore comes from a Javanese account, the *Nagarakretagama*, which referred to a settlement called Temasek (Sea Town) on the island.

Chinese trade ships traveling between the South China Sea and the Strait of Malacca in Malaysia would break their journey at this conveniently located place. Early travelers' accounts describe it as a wild place, where piracy was a way of life.

By the 13th century, Temasek had a new name, Singapura, or "Lion City." A century later, Singapore was caught up in the prolonged conflict between Siam (Thailand) and the Java-based Majapahit empire for control of the Malay Peninsula. A victim of the conflict, Singapore fell into decay and was to lie dormant until its reawakening in the early 19th century.

An artist's impression of an early Singapore port.

According to tradition, an Indian king, Raja Chulan, married a mermaid and had three sons, who later became rulers of kingdoms in Sumatra. The youngest, Sang Nila Utama, searched the nearby islands as possible sites for a new city and was particularly attracted by one. It was called Temasek.

As Sang Nila Utama and his men sailed toward the island, their ship was caught in a fierce storm and began to sink. To lighten their load, Sang Nila Utama threw his crown into the sea. Suddenly the sea became calm, and the men reached Temasek's shores in safety. While exploring the island, they saw a strange animal. Sang Nila Utama was told that it was a lion.

Seeing such a strong, bold creature was a good omen. The king believed he had found the place to build a great city and decided to call it Singapura, "Lion City."

EARLY HISTORY

Singapore became prominent in about 1390, when Parameswara, a prince of Palembang in Sumatra, set himself up as ruler of the island after murdering his host, the chieftain. Soon after, however, he was driven out in the struggle between neighboring countries for control of the Malay Peninsula. Parameswara fled to Malacca (known as Melaka in Malay), where he founded the powerful Malacca sultanate.

In the early 16th century, Malacca was captured by the Portuguese, and the sultan escaped farther south to set up a new kingdom, the sultanate Johor-Riau, which included Singapore. An outpost was established on the island only to be burned down by the Portuguese.

Traders and seamen subsequently deserted the island, leaving it once again to pirates and Malay people called Orang Laut. A few Malays and Chinese from the Riau Islands and some Orang Laut formed a village settlement (called a kampong in Malay) by the Singapore River, led by a *temenggong* (ter-meng-gong), a senior minister of the Johor-Riau Sultanate.

On January 2, 1819, a British fleet led by Sir Thomas Stamford Raffles arrived on the island. It wanted to set up a trading post. The *temenggong*

When Raffles first arrived in 1819, Singapore was a small settlement of about 150 people. In 1824, Malays made up nearly three-quarters of the population. By 1867, however, the Chinese had firmly established themselves as the majority. In the 19th century there were almost no women on the island, but today there is a fairly even division between the sexes. Since 1980, official population figures have been calculated on the basis of Singapore citizens and permanent residents only. In 2010 this was estimated at more than 5.1 million people, made up of 74.1 percent Chinese, 13.4 percent Malay, and 9.2 percent Indians, with a small group of mixed ethnicity. Living among the population are a large number of foreign domestic servants and other workers.

and the young sultan of Johor could not give their consent; by then the Dutch had control of Malacca and the sultanate. However, the British proclaimed an elder brother the rightful sultan, and permission was granted through him instead. A ceremony followed to raise the British flag and mark the founding of modern Singapore.

POLITICAL HISTORY

Raffles thought Singapore the perfect answer to the British need for a port in the south of the Malay Peninsula. It would protect merchant ships in the area and prevent the Dutch from gaining additional power over the lucrative East Indian spice trade.

In 1826 the British added Singapore to two other ports on the Malay Peninsula, Malacca and Penang, forming the Straits Settlements. All three were governed by the British government in India until 1867, when they became a single crown colony and were governed by the Colonial Office in London.

In 1914 all the Malay states, including the Straits Settlements, came under British rule as British Malaya. This led to peace, an improvement in government, and trade between the rest of Malaya and Singapore. In 1923 a linking causeway and railway were built to extend these commercial ties.

The arrival of the steamship and the opening of the Suez Canal in 1869 made Singapore once again an important stopover for ships traveling between Europe and East Asia. At this time the island enjoyed unprecedented prosperity.

THE JAPANESE OCCUPATION   During World War II the Japanese wanted control over Southeast Asia's reserves of oil, rubber, tin, and other supplies. This prompted the Japanese capture of Singapore in February 1942, a brutal occupation lasting three and a half years. During this time, there was little foreign trade, resulting in poor business, high unemployment, and a shortage of food and medicine. It was a period of great hardship that resulted in a longing to be free from foreign rule.

A print of Chinese traders from the Straits Settlements around the 1800s.

THE COMMUNIST INSURGENCY   When the Japanese surrendered in 1945, the British returned to Singapore. In the meantime, anti-Japanese groups had turned anti-British. Communists gained the support of students and workers and used them to provoke strikes and riots. In 1948 a state of emergency against communism was called that lasted until 1960.

A British governor and his advisers ruled the Straits Settlements separately from the rest of Malaya. This met with fierce opposition from local leaders due to Singapore's close commercial ties with the mainland. In 1955 new political parties and partial self-government marked the first move toward democracy. By 1959 Singapore had a government led by its own prime minister and his cabinet, although it remained under British control.

GAINING INDEPENDENCE   In September 1963 the British declared that Singapore merge with a group of Malayan territories to form the Federation of Malaysia. This was meant to expand the country's economy and enable it to be free of British rule. Singapore and Malaysia disagreed on many issues, however, particularly those concerning race, and Singapore left the federation after two years. It became an independent country on August 9, 1965. Many in Singapore, including its leader, Lee Kuan Yew, were unsure if this small nation with no natural resources would survive.

SINGAPORE TODAY   Since gaining independence in 1965, the people of Singapore and its leaders were determined to make their new nation a commercial and economic success. The country embarked on a major industrialization program of building and modernizing its infrastructure, including its telecommunication systems, public housing, roads, port, and airport. Singapore revamped its education system and declared English the official language in order to promote communication among the races and to facilitate international trade. This ambitious program was incredibly successful, and by the late 1980s Singapore had moved from a vulnerable country to a thriving one with a well-developed economy.

General Percival, British commander of Singapore (carrying flag), on his way to surrender to the Japanese in 1942.

SOCIAL HISTORY

After the British set up a trading post in 1819, Singapore's newfound prosperity brought a huge influx of people from all over the region in search of work, trade, or an escape from warring conditions in their homelands. Immigration brought badly needed cheap labor, marking the beginning of Singapore's multiracial society.

The population increased rapidly, leading to new settlements in other parts of the island. The town became increasingly crowded, dirty, and disorganized, hindering its growth as an important city. Raffles drew up a plan dividing the city into a series of districts. He set aside a government

SECRET SOCIETIES

When Chinese immigrants first arrived in Singapore, they often joined secret societies to combat poverty and loneliness. In return for work and lodging, they had to obey specific rules and often became involved in gang fights or in the collection of "protection" money. Members who broke the rules were severely punished.

The Chinese Protectorate was set up in 1877 under William Pickering, a much respected man who both spoke and wrote various Chinese dialects. He was able to help the government deal with these secret societies until a law was passed to suppress the largest of them.

Other Chinese immigrants joined together in clans—friendly societies of people who came from the same district in China and shared a common dialect. Clan associations served the social needs of their members, most of whom had no families in Singapore. These groups kept the immigrants in touch with people like themselves, who helped one another in times of trouble. Many of these clans survive to this day. They have evolved to meet the changing needs of their members, providing scholarships and classes to teach Chinese culture and customs, which help to make the younger generation aware of its heritage.

area on the south bank and a commercial area for merchants and traders in the north, and resettled the main ethnic groups in separate residential areas along the coast.

In spite of these improvements, slum conditions prevailed, and tropical diseases were rampant. The death rate was high, although by the early 20th century some public health services were provided, and philanthropists had built hospitals for the poor. The Japanese occupation and the steady rise in population caused living conditions to deteriorate, and town planning was reintroduced in the late 1940s under the Singapore Improvement Trust. By the 1960s the Housing and Development Board (HDB) was set up to provide public housing on a large scale and to make the surrounding environment more attractive. Today 85 percent of the population lives in modern public housing, mostly in high-rise apartments, provided by the HDB.

"Our object is not territory but trade, a commercial emporium..."
—Sir Stamford Raffles, founder of Singapore

THE FALL OF SINGAPORE

The surrender of Singapore to the Japanese army, known as the Fall of Singapore, on February 15, 1942, is considered one of the British army's most shameful defeats of World War II. This momentous event, which followed the bombing of Pearl Harbor in December 1941, confirmed the power of the Japanese army.

Based on its location at the end of the Malay Peninsula, Singapore was considered an impregnable fortress by the British rulers. The British were confident that the Japanese would attack from the sea, so they established their defenses accordingly. The Japanese took everyone by surprise, however, by taking the more difficult route and attacking through the jungles of the Malay Peninsula. The Japanese eventually entered Singapore on bicycles through the causeway that links the Malay Peninsula to Singapore.

The British army of 90,000 men, lead by Lieutenant General Arthur Percival, tried to defend Singapore, but the element of surprise combined with the speed and brutality of the Japanese attack made this a challenging task. The British army was forced to retreat. It would seem that the British had underestimated the ability and effectiveness of the Japanese army and paid dearly for their complacency. The Japanese occupied Singapore until 1945.

INTERNET LINKS

www.postcolonialweb.org/singapore/history/historyov.html

A website examining Singapore's colonial past and fall during World War II.

http://countrystudies.us/singapore/10.htm

A brief overview of the history of Singapore—in particular, the rise and role of the now-dominant political party, the People's Action Party, as well as Singapore's split from the Federation of Malaysia.

GOVERNMENT

The parliament building in Singapore.

3

SINGAPORE'S LONG RULE BY THE British East India Company in the 19th century laid the foundations for its future government.

Sir Thomas Stamford Raffles set up the first modern-day laws, and Singapore's governmental system remains based on the British system, although it has been modified to meet the special requirements of a multiracial people. Government philosophy is also influenced by the Chinese system of ethics known as Confucianism.

NATIONAL GOVERNMENT

Singapore is a republic and has a parliamentary system based on the British House of Commons, with a parliamentary act that states its

The president of Singapore, S.R. Nathan, delivering a speech at Keio University in Tokyo.

The head of the government of Singapore is the prime minister. The head of state is the president, who has the power to veto decisions made by the cabinet. The ruling party, the People's Action Party, was founded by Minister Mentor Lee Kuan Yew, who was also Singapore's first prime minister. The last elections held in Singapore were in 2011.

powers and restrictions. The president of Singapore used to be elected by parliament but since 1993 has been elected by the citizens to hold office for six years. The first president elected by the people was Ong Teng Cheong, who served from 1993 to 1999. The current president of Singapore is Sellapan Ramanathan, also known as S.R. Nathan, who came to office on August 18, 1999.

The president is head of state and appoints a member of parliament as prime minister and a group of ministers to form the cabinet. Each minister is responsible for a different ministry, such as the Ministry of Defense, Law, and Education. The prime minister is the head of government, but under the recent constitutional changes, the elected president has important powers of veto over some decisions made by the parliament. The president, in consultation with the Presidential Council of Advisers, is responsible for appointing key civil servants.

Prime Minister Lee Hsien Loong was elected in 2004.

The People's Action Party (PAP), formed on multiracial principles, was founded in 1954 and has remained in power since its historic election in 1959. Its first leader, Lee Kuan Yew, probably exercised more influence over the people and saw more of his dreams for the country become a reality than any other head of government in the world.

Opposition to the PAP government exists, but there has been a lack of unity among those who oppose it. The government has often been criticized for its strict control over the print and broadcast media, including the circulation of magazines. As the government insists on its right to reply to criticism published in publications, there has also been a series of conflicts with leading international newspapers and magazines.

Once Singapore became an independent nation in 1965, its citizens had to think of themselves as Singaporeans rather than British subjects or Malaysians. Sensitivity to issues of ideology, race, and language that

Supporters of opposition party, the Workers' Party, show their support for their party's candidate during the 2006 elections.

divided society became crucial to the success of the new nation. Even with stability and prosperity, Singapore continues to search for a national ideology, a set of traditional values common to each community yet relevant to a modern society.

Singapore's most recent election was held on May 7, 2011. The 2011 elections saw 82 out of 87 seats contested, the highest number of seats contested since the country's independence. The opposition party, The Worker's Party, claimed six parliamentary seats. Despite the PAP's success, opposition parties saw an overall increase in vote share percentages as compared to previous elections.

The aftermath of the 2011 elections saw a radical re-shuffle in Singapore's cabinet, where three veteran ministers, Wong Kan Seng, Raymond Lim and Mah Bow Tan, stepped down. Also missing from the cabinet was foreign minister George Yeo, who had lost in the elections. Minister Mentor Lee

Supporters of the ruling party, the People's Action Party, waving party flags after the PAP was returned to power in 2006 elections.

Kuan Yew and Senior Minister Goh Chok Tong also stepped down from their positions in the cabinet.

LOCAL AUTHORITIES

Singapore has many public housing developments built by a government agency, the HDB. In each town there are apartment blocks, schools, shopping facilities that range from markets to modern department stores, community centers, and factories. All these facilities make the new towns self-supporting. The town councils and residents' committees manage and maintain the public housing developments. These committees act as a channel through which decisions for the residents can be made at a local level. A government liaison officer maintains links with the residents' committees to make sure the public is kept in touch with national policies.

Blocks of public housing apartments in Singapore. Located near these apartments are facilities and amenities such as supermarkets, libraries, and public transport.

Lee Kuan Yew was the first and longest-serving prime minister of the Republic of Singapore, from 1959 to 1990. He served Singapore as a mentor minister and remains an important and inspiring political figure in the region. He stepped down from the cabinet following the 2011 elections.

He founded the ruling PAP and has been credited with the economic miracle of Singapore, which transformed a fragile country with no natural resources into one of the most developed countries in Southeast Asia and the world.

Born on September 16, 1923, the first child of a Singaporean-Chinese family, Lee Kuan Yew was educated at Raffles Institution and Raffles College before earning a law degree from prestigious Cambridge University in the United Kingdom. He married in 1950 and has three children. His eldest son, Lee Hsien Loong, is the current prime minister of Singapore.

Lee Kuan Yew's political life began in 1951, and by 1954 he had formed the PAP. The PAP won a landslide victory in its first national elections in 1959, and Lee was elected prime minister. Between 1962 and 1965, Lee played a pivotal role in Singapore's merger with Malaysia and, subsequently, its expulsion from the Federation of Malaysia. The separation of Singapore from the federation was a terrible blow to Lee, who very much felt it was a personal failure. He was fearful that Singapore was too vulnerable and lacking in resources to manage on its own. However, the shock of the expulsion motivated him to make Singapore survive, and the success story that is Singapore today is a testament to his hard work, sheer determination, and vision.

Although criticized by some for his authoritarian style, Lee Kuan Yew is widely respected by both the younger and older generations of Singaporeans, who believe they owe him much of their economic prosperity and national stability.

LEGAL STRUCTURES

Administration of justice is in the hands of the supreme court and the subordinate courts. An attorney general and his legal officers advise the government on legal matters and perform legal duties assigned to them by the cabinet.

The supreme court consists of the chief justice and judges appointed by the president on the advice of the prime minister. The subordinate courts consist of district judges, magistrates, coroners, and small-claims referees who are appointed by the president on the recommendation of the chief justice.

The death sentence is enforced in Singapore for trafficking in narcotics. Strict rules and rigorous government campaigns are regularly imposed on the public, and some may appear unnecessarily restrictive to individual freedom. However, many Singaporeans regard these regulations simply as the government's response to national needs.

INTERNET LINKS

www.lee-kuan-yew.com/
A collection of Internet links to articles and interviews about and with Minister Mentor Lee Kuan Yew. It also contains a list of books about and by Lee Kuan Yew.

http://yoursdp.org/
A look at the activities of the Singapore Democratic Party. It also offers a different perspective on issues that affect Singaporeans.

http://countrystudies.us/singapore/55.htm
This website presents a brief but comprehensive look at the various opposition parties in Singapore.

ECONOMY

An aerial view of the Singapore Port. Singapore is the world's busiest transshipment port.

4

SINGAPORE, HONG KONG, South Korea, and Taiwan make up the Four Asian Tigers, also called the Asian Dragons. Singapore has an advanced economy that has consistently experienced high levels of growth since the 1960s.

The country is well known for its relatively corruption-free government and business environment. The economy relies on exports, in particular consumer electronics, information technology products, and pharmaceuticals. The financial services sector is also becoming

A container ship docking in Singapore.

an important part of the economy. The way in which Singapore's economy operates is unique and has been referred to by economists as "the Singapore model." This can be defined as a free-market economy combined with extensive government control and planning.

The World Bank "Doing Business 2010 Report" rated the Singapore economy as having the most open and liberal economy for international trade. It also ranked Singapore second for investment potential, and first in Asia and fourth in the world for low levels of corruption.

As Singapore has no natural resources worth exploiting other than its harbor and strategic location, its main resource is its people. When the first immigrants settled on the island of Singapore, they tended to fall into specific occupational groups. The bulk of the Chinese were traders and businessmen, the Malays were fishermen and farmers, and the Indians were merchants and moneylenders.

Over the years the population grew rapidly. Jobs were created to employ a great many people, especially when it became clear that Singapore needed to produce goods that would be in demand in developed countries.

The financial district in Singapore. Many global companies set up their regional offices in Singapore due to its stable economy and educated workforce.

Today the largest group of workers are employed in the services industry. The labor force consists of more than 3 million workers; 76.2 percent are employed in the services sector and 23.8 percent in the industry sector. Large businesses in fields including banking, insurance, and manufacturing have created a rise in financial and business services. Singapore's location, efficient trading links, educated workforce, and political stability have attracted large foreign companies with a network of international markets.

To encourage more entrepreneurial Singaporeans to establish and expand their businesses, the government's Economic Development Board has set up several aid programs, such as the Innovation Development Scheme, the Research Incentive Scheme for Companies, and Initiatives for New Technology.

INDUSTRIES

When Singapore became independent in 1965, it became clear, due to its lack of natural resources, that it needed to produce goods that would be

Factory workers checking digital video disc (DVD) players on the assembly line.

An oil refinery in Singapore. Singapore refines crude oil before exporting it to other countries.

in demand in developed countries. Large-scale manufacturing industries were started, and these became the source of Singapore's success. A large percentage of workers had to be trained to handle the specialized equipment. Today there is no shortage of skilled workers, the result of investment in technical education.

The island is becoming increasingly attractive to Japanese and U.S. corporations that plan to install their operational headquarters overseas. The importance of this to Singapore lies not just in the employment generated but also in the technology and skills its workers can learn.

The republic is the most important oil-refining center in Southeast Asia and one of the largest in the world. Crude oil is brought to Singapore from Malaysia, Brunei, Indonesia, and the Middle East, refined into many grades for different purposes, and exported. Japan, Hong Kong, Malaysia, Australia, and Thailand buy most of the oil, but some is retained to fuel power stations and local transportation. Gas production and sales have increased in recent years; Singapore imports its natural gas from Malaysia and Indonesia via four offshore pipelines.

The manufacturing sector, in particular electronics, is the mainstay of the economy. Industries include the manufacture of color televisions, calculators, radios, computers, and electronic medical instruments.

In the past low-value goods were produced, but the presence of international companies meant higher-quality goods could now be produced and exported. This has shifted the emphasis to high-technology, high-value products such as aircraft components and oil-rig construction.

A medical researcher conducting research at the Biopolis in Singapore.

Light industry includes clothing manufacturing, food processing, and the manufacture of household utensils, most of which is carried out in industrial parks.

To diversify its economy, Singapore has been investing heavily in building a biotechnology and biomedical industry, in particular the manufacturing and production of pharmaceuticals. Today pharmaceuticals contribute 16 percent of Singapore's manufacturing output. Millions have been spent on attracting top scientists from abroad to work in Singapore, developing the appropriate infrastructure, and making funds for research available.

Apart from the manufacturing of pharmaceuticals, Singapore is also promoting itself as a center for research in the biomedical fields. Already more than 50 companies are carrying out biomedical research and development projects including drug discovery, translational research, and clinical research.

In Singapore today there are seven research institutes and five research consortia in key fields including clinical sciences, genomics, bioengineering, cell biology, medical biology, bioimaging, and immunology. In 2008 the Cancer Research Centre of Excellence and the Centre for Translational

Tourism contributes 3 percent to Singapore's gross domestic product (GDP). In 2009, 9.7 million people visited the republic. The Singapore Tourism Board (STB) aims to increase the role tourism plays in the country's economy by attracting twice as many visitors by 2015. This would generate revenue as well as create thousands of jobs.

Besides promoting Singapore as a leisure destination, the STB also plans to promote it as an ideal business destination for conventions and exhibitions. Singapore already promotes itself as a center for medical tourism. It has been estimated that around 200,000 visitors, attracted to its excellent medical care and world-class hospital facilities, come to the country in search of medical treatment.

Medicine were established. Singapore has been successful in attracting many major pharmaceutical companies including GlaxoSmithKline, Pfizer, Abbott, AstraZeneca, Bayer, Boehringer-Ingelheim, Bristol-Myers Squibb, Genzyme, Merck Sharp & Dohme, Quintiles, Roche, and Sanofi-aventis, some of whom have their own plants in Singapore.

Singapore has built its biomedical industry by partnering with international pharmaceutical firms and top scientists from abroad. It has also developed its own successful local firms such as MerLion Pharmaceuticals, which received the Scrip Award for Best Company in an Emerging Market in 2007.

COTTAGE INDUSTRIES

Few of the cottage industries of old Singapore survive, and it is only a matter of time before they disappear forever. The business problems of the Indian garland maker are typical: Demand for the garlands exists, but mechanization cannot help, and no one is willing to do such repetitive work for so many hours daily. The starting pay, often with lodging and food included, compares well with that offered elsewhere, but young people are uninterested in keeping up a tradition that offers no recognition or opportunity for progress. They prefer to train for something more professional.

The man who wheels a trolley full of homemade festival masks and the woman who designs and sews patchwork quilts are growing old, and there is no one to pass their skills to. Some trades such as pottery or joss-stick making involve whole families who have passed on the tradition for generations. But most younger people prefer to work in air-conditioned offices.

SOURCES OF REVENUE

Singapore is an entrepôt port, which means that goods such as printed circuits or telecommunications apparatus are imported from abroad and then exported to other countries. Other exports are goods manufactured in Singapore for sale overseas, including office machines, radio and television receivers, computers, and electronic components. Almost three-quarters of the clothing made in Singapore is exported.

Singapore has the busiest port in the world, coping efficiently with huge amounts of ocean traffic and cargo 24 hours a day. It is a major port for passenger liners plying to and from Australia, Europe, the United States,

A cruise ship docking in a port in Singapore.

India, and Hong Kong; a destination for oil tankers from the Middle East; and a docking station for ships in need of repair.

Singapore's Changi Airport is one of the busiest in the region. It has also repeatedly won awards for its high level of service and excellent facilities.

In an attempt to generate 35,000 jobs and promote further economic growth, the government offered approval for the first-ever licensed casinos to be opened in the republic. These casinos would operate within the concept of an "integrated resort," or IR, which would provide family entertainment and business convention facilities as well. Two integrated resorts, Marina Bay Sands, and Resorts World Sentosa, opened in 2010.

Singapore has tapped into other ways of boosting its economy including hosting large-scale international events such as the first Formula 1 night race in 2007 and the inaugural Youth Olympic Games in 2010.

The Marina Bay Sands, an integrated resort, hosts not only casinos but also family entertainment and shopping, right in the heart of Singapore.

WORK ETHIC

Singapore's progress owes much to its work ethic, a striving for excellence with money as motivation and personal success as the goal. But in some areas, concern has been expressed about high staff turnover.

Singaporeans work long hours, driven hard by a government and an education system that expect them to excel. Today's workers are better educated and better trained, and therefore more assertive than their predecessors. The increasingly competitive environment among employers may create even better conditions for local workers. More Singapore companies are looking for markets in other countries, such as China, Malaysia, and Indonesia, and a move has been made to encourage managers and experts to spend time overseas.

AN IMPORTED WORKFORCE

Singapore depends to a great extent on a foreign workforce, as its economy continues to grow, and new jobs are created each year. In 2006 there were 580,000 unskilled or low-skilled foreign workers and 90,000 skilled "foreign talents." The government actively recruits foreign talent—professionals, engineers, and entrepreneurs—from other Asian countries such as India and China to fill the gap.

Among the foreign workers, unskilled workers form a large proportion, doing jobs that Singaporeans are less willing to undertake—domestic maids, construction workers, production-line workers, and manual laborers. They come from poorer Asian countries such as the Philippines, India, Thailand, and Indonesia. On Sunday afternoons they get together in large groups by nationality in favored gathering places to chat and enjoy their day off. Singaporeans acknowledge that their economy is heavily reliant on a foreign workforce.

INTERNET LINKS

http://app.mti.gov.sg/default.asp?id=1

This is the website of Singapore's Ministry of Trade and Industry. It aims to promote economic growth and create employment.

www.worldbank.org/sg

Learn about the World Bank in Singapore and its activities throughout Southeast Asia.

www.nationsencyclopedia.com/Asia-and-Oceania/Singapore-ECONOMIC-DEVELOPMENT.html

A brief but concise look at Singapore's economic development until the early 2000s.

ENVIRONMENT

People strolling in the Singapore Botanic Gardens.

5

AS SINGAPORE IS A SMALL NATION, only 269 square miles (697 square km) in area, the impact of its growing population on the land has been dramatic. There is little of the island that has not been urbanized.

Sir Thomas Stamford Raffles, the founder of modern Singapore, would certainly not recognize his city today. The tiny city-state has expanded significantly through land reclamation, and there is hardly an area not filled with houses, apartment buildings, industrial parks, or high-rise office buildings. All these are linked by a highly developed system of roads and expressways and a rapid mass-transit train system.

Due to Singapore's small land size and high population, most of the island is built up.

Despite the pressure of high population density, the quality of life in Singapore as reflected in the environment is excellent. Actions taken by the government ensure that the environment and the health of the people are safeguarded.

The Singapore government has signed the following international agreements: Biodiversity, Climate Change, Kyoto Protocol, Desertification, Endangered Species, Hazardous Wastes, Law of the Sea, Ozone Layer Protection, and Ship Pollution.

GREEN LUNGS

Singapore could very easily have become an ugly, smog-ridden city had it not been for the foresight of government leaders. They were concerned that the rapid growth and urbanization of the land would lead to a lack of greenery. So they made a point of ensuring that there would be parks and gardens everywhere. These are the "green lungs" of the city.

Pasir Ris Park is one of the many parks in Singapore.

NATURE RESERVES

There is very little of Singapore's forests that have not been cleared or otherwise disturbed. Together with the elimination of primary forests, large wildlife has disappeared. Recognizing this, the National Parks Board has made several areas of the island into nature reserves to preserve what is left for birds and other small wildlife as well as for the enjoyment and education of Singaporeans.

The 406-acre (164 ha) Bukit Timah Nature Reserve is in the heart of the island and includes Bukit Timah Hill, which at 538 feet (164 m) tall is the highest point in Singapore. The reserve has the only large area of primary rain forest in the country and has a rich diversity of plant species. Small animals such as the plantain squirrel, the long-tailed macaque, the flying lemur, and the common tree shrew live in the reserve. The bird's-nest fern, the resam fern, and the liana flourish in the wet and warm equatorial climate, adding texture to the forms of large trees.

Sungei Buloh Nature Park, along the northwestern coast of the island, is an area of mangrove swamps, mudflats, and brackish ponds. It is an important stopping and refueling point for migratory birds that come from as far north as Siberia and China. It is also home to resident birds such as the heron, the kingfisher, the bee-eater, the woodpecker, and the munia.

Pulau Ubin (pictured) is an island off the northeastern coast of Singapore. Its few inhabitants maintain a slow kampong, or village, lifestyle to give visitors a taste of what Singapore must have been like in the 1950s and 1960s. Many of the abandoned gardens and farms have been returned to nature.

The Lower Peirce Trail is easily accessible to visitors, being just a few minutes away from the city. Tall rain-forest trees, numerous flowering plants, ferns, and small animals are features of this nature reserve.

Today the National Parks Board is responsible for developing and maintaining Singapore's reputation as a green city. There are thousands of acres (hectares) of parks and green open spaces, both publicly and privately owned. The Singapore Botanic Gardens and Fort Canning Park are two large sanctuaries in the heart of the city. There are many other parks and gardens for recreation, and trees and shrubbery line the city's vast network of roads. The Parks Board plans to link major parks and nature reserves to provide green corridors with cycling and walking trails.

In northern Singapore is the Bukit Timah Nature Reserve. Other nature reserves include Pulau Ubin, Sungei Buloh Nature Park, and Labrador Park.

THE AIR WE BREATHE

Stringent laws ensure that the quality of air in Singapore is monitored and pollution from industries and vehicles is controlled. The amount of pollutants in the air, such as sulfur dioxide and nitrogen dioxide, is closely watched. While the thousands of vehicles traveling the roads can cause traffic jams

Heavy traffic along Orchard Road in Singapore.

HAZY DAYS

Despite the fact that Singapore does its best to control the amount of pollutants in the air, its close proximity to the larger countries of Indonesia and Malaysia means that it is very vulnerable to the activities in these countries. This was most evident to everyone in 1997, 2006, and 2010—years that forest fires raged uncontrollably in Indonesia. The fires had deliberately been set by big logging and plantation companies in order to clear the land. Although this had been the practice for many years, a practice that often caused a haze over Singapore skies, it had never been as bad as in 1997. That year, the rains that usually douse the fires from July to October were delayed. During the time of the fires Singaporeans woke up to a strange smell in the air, the sun was a red ball in the sky, the outline of city buildings could hardly be seen, and health warnings were constantly issued to urge people to remain indoors if they could. Firefighters all over the world were sent to Indonesia to help put out the fires. The licenses of more than 150 companies in Indonesia were revoked, but many have since been reinstated. In 2010, Singapore was again covered in thick smoke and saw its three-hour Pollutant Standard Index recording rise to an unhealthy range of 108, the worst recording since the haze of 2006.

and pollute the air, it is rare to see a beat-up old clunker of a car belching black, ugly fumes from its exhaust. This is because the quality of fuel used in vehicles is controlled to reduce emissions of noxious gases into the atmosphere, and the majority of vehicles are in good condition; few are more than 10 years old. People have to pay huge amounts of taxes to be entitled to buy a vehicle. If they want to use a car that is considered too old, it costs them even more money. As a result, most vehicles that are no longer roadworthy are scrapped.

EVERY DROP COUNTS

Water is an extremely scarce resource in Singapore. Currently Singapore receives water from four main sources: 20 percent comes from the 14 reservoirs on the island, 40 percent is imported from the neighboring Malaysian state of Johor, 30 percent is reclaimed water (wastewater that has been purified), and 10 percent comes from desalination of seawater. As of 2008 there were five water reclamation plants dotted throughout the island, producing about 50 million gallons (189 million liters) of water per day.

The government would like to become less reliant on Malaysia for water. Thus, in 1991, it signed a 50-year agreement with Indonesia to develop water sources in the nearby Indonesian province of Riau.

Although water is scarce in Singapore, management of the water supply is outstanding. Every Singaporean has easy access to clean, safe, and inexpensive water. Singapore's water reclamation and desalination programs have been so successful that in 2007, Singapore's Public Utilities Board received the Stockholm Industry Water Award.

An engineer making routine checks at the NEWater plant in Singapore. NEWater utilizes advanced water purification technology to turn wastewater into potable water.

HEALTH AND FOOD HYGIENE

Another environmental improvement has been the reduction and elimination of many diseases that plague other tropical countries, such as yellow fever, cholera, and typhoid fever. There are a few cases each year of malaria, dengue fever, and other diseases carried by insects, but stringent checks and monitoring keep these under control. Mosquitoes are more of an irritant than a health hazard. A bite brings no more discomfort than a red welt on the skin and an itch.

The Ministry of the Environment and Water Resources does its best to keep in check the number of mosquitoes and other disease-carrying creatures such as cockroaches, flies, and rats. Because Singaporeans are extremely fond of eating out, hygiene at the numerous food and hawker centers all over the island is an important health concern. Food sellers and their stalls are regularly checked for the quality of their cleanliness. They are rated accordingly—A, B, and C—and have to display these ratings prominently so that buyers are informed.

INTERNET LINKS

www.circleofblue.org/waternews/2011/world/bottling-wastewater-expands-island%E2%80%99s-oasis%E2%80%94singapore%E2%80%99s-newater-solution-to-scarcity/

An interesting article about Singapore's use of NEWater. It also highlights the filtration and treatment systems used.

http://app.nea.gov.sg/cms/htdocs/category_sub.asp?cid=40

Learn about the campaigns and programs that Singapore runs to educate the public about environmental issues.

www.eco-singapore.org

A not-for-profit organization that seeks to encourage young Singaporeans to lead more environmentally responsible lives through programs and events.

SINGAPOREANS

An Indian woman with her child in Little India.
There are four main ethnic groups in Singapore.

BY THE TIME SIR STAMFORD RAFFLES landed in Singapore, a small number of Malays and Chinese had already arrived from nearby settlements ruled by the Dutch. The Malays were followed by the Javanese, the Bugis, and the Balinese from Indonesia, people with a similar lifestyle who were mainly traders and integrated well with the Malays.

The few Chinese worked on gambier and pepper plantations, but the opening up of trading opportunities brought a huge influx of people from

There are four main ethnic groups in Singapore: the Chinese, the Eurasians, the Indians, and the Malays. While each group is encouraged to hold on to their own culture and traditional practices, locals are reminded that they are, above all, Singaporeans.

Singaporeans enjoying a leisurely bicycle ride in East Coast Park.

many parts of China. Most were laborers and craftspeople who specialized in certain trades. These made up Singapore's four main Chinese dialect groups—the Hokkiens, the Teochews, the Cantonese, and the Hakkas—whose members settled in separate districts of Chinatown on the south bank of the Singapore River.

Opportunities for work as clerks, technicians, teachers, merchants, and moneylenders brought Indian immigrants from Malaysia, India, and Sri Lanka. In the early 19th century, Singapore became a penal colony for Indian convicts whose labor was needed to build public housing and what were to become Singapore's finest churches and temples. The British also brought in laborers under contract for certain periods to build roads, railways, bridges, and waterways. The first census, in 1824, recorded a population of 11,000. By 1871 the population had risen to 97,000, and by 1900 to 228,000.

Today the Singapore population of more than 5.1 million is completely urbanized. The republic has a young population—almost 74 percent are

A group of Singaporean boys enjoy a day at the beach. While Singapore has many young people, it is also experiencing a graying population.

between the ages of 15 and 64 years. The median age is 37.4 years old. Life expectancy is a healthy 82 years.

MAIN ETHNIC GROUPS

By 1860 three-fourths of the population was Chinese. Indians made up the second-largest group, followed by Malays, Arabs, Eurasians, and Europeans. Even though the society was multicultural, it was made up almost entirely of men. Toward the end of the 19th century, women were encouraged to join them, after which many of the immigrants chose to settle in Singapore permanently. According to the 2010 census estimates, the Chinese make up 74.1 percent of the population, Malays 13.4 percent, Indians 9.2 percent, and others 3.3 percent.

THE CHINESE The first Chinese settlement as designated by Raffles was Chinatown, a large area south of the Singapore River. Chinatown itself

Elderly women in Chinatown. The life expectancy of Singaporeans is a robust 82 years.

was further divided into separate areas for the different dialect groups, each with a headman to prevent fighting among themselves.

The Chinese who originally settled in Singapore were migrants in search of a new life, poor people who were prepared to work very hard to make their fortune. Although those born and bred in Singapore today may feel no ties to a homeland they have never seen, many still hold fast to the work ethic brought over by their forefathers.

THE MALAYS They are the second-largest ethnic group and possibly Singapore's original inhabitants. Of the early settlers, the Bugis, former pirates from Sulawesi; the Boyanese from Madura in Indonesia; and the Orang Laut, descendants of sea gypsies, have all been absorbed into the Malay culture.

The Malays are a warm and hospitable people united by a common faith, Islam, that pervades their lives. Though they originally lived in fishing villages,

A group of Malay students on a field trip.

A group of Indians in Little India.

they have adapted to city life. Separated from the large Malay communities that extend from the Philippines to Thailand, they are developing their own identity as Singaporeans.

THE INDIANS These immigrants originally considered Singapore a temporary base where they could make money to send home. It was only later that they brought their families and settled permanently.

Tamils from South India make up about 80 percent of the Indian population, but there are also people from other parts of the Indian subcontinent living in Singapore. These include Gujaratis, Punjabis, Bengalis, Sindhis, Sri Lankan Tamils, and Sinhalese. Perhaps because of their now-fading links with India, Singaporean Indians are a close community, careful to preserve their old customs among the variety of cultural influences surrounding them.

THE EURASIANS This important minority group consists mainly of people of Asian and Portuguese origin from Goa and Malacca. They settled easily in Singapore, as intermarriage has always been socially acceptable.

THE SINGAPOREAN IDENTITY

Ever since Singapore gained independence in the 1960s, the government has been trying to forge a unique Singaporean identity based on the Asian values of family and hard work. Unlike the American concept of a melting pot, the Singaporean identity encompasses the idea of multiculturalism whereby all three main ethnicities—Chinese, Indian, and Malay—live together in peace and harmony. Whatever ethnicity a Singaporean belongs to, he or she knows to respect other ethnic groups' customs, languages, and religions.

The official language of English binds every Singaporean and facilitates communication and understanding. In schools across the republic, children begin their day by singing the national anthem and reciting the Singapore national pledge. The words of the pledge are as follows:

> We, the citizens of Singapore,
> pledge ourselves as one united people,
> regardless of race, language, or religion,
> to build a democratic society
> based on justice and equality
> so as to achieve happiness, prosperity, and
> progress for our nation.

NAMES

Chinese people usually have two "given" names and a "family" name, which is placed first. If a man is called Lim See Teo, he is known as Mr. Lim. His wife will retain her father's family name, although she will also be known as Mrs. Lim. Many Singaporean Chinese adopt a Western name as well, either because they become Christians or because they associate Western names with being more modern.

Malay family names do not last more than one generation. The second generation adds their father's name to the end of their own name. Mr. Jaafar Abdullah may be called Jaafar or Mr. Jaafar. Abdullah was his father's name.

Many of the early Chinese emigrants to Malaya and Singapore married Malay women. The result was a separate community of people referred to as the Straits-born Chinese, or Peranakans , which means "locally born."

The Peranakans considered themselves very different from the true Chinese, developing their own unique culture. After many centuries they evolved a language of their own, Baba Malay, a mixture of Malay and the Chinese Hokkien dialect. At the same time, they were among the first people in the area to learn English and pick up Western customs.

As the Peranakans become absorbed into the wider population, there is an effort to keep their culture and customs alive. Their unique cuisine is enjoyed by everyone, plays celebrate their familial customs, and many books have been written about their social history and colorful costumes and art.

His son, Ahmad, will be known as Ahmad Jaafar. *Bin* or *binte*, meaning "son of" or "daughter of" respectively, may be included between these names—for example, Ahmad bin Jaafar—but is often dropped these days.

Tamil Singaporeans do not have true family names either. They use the initial of their father's name placed before their own (for example, S. Ramasamy), or they use it as a surname (such as Ramasamy Suppiah). A Tamil woman will not use her father's name when she gets married but will become simply Mrs. Ramasamy.

All the ethnic groups have distinct titles for each family relationship. Children in the United States use the same word, *grandfather*, to refer to their father's or mother's father. In Singapore, the term will vary depending on whose father it is—the mother's father or the father's father. This distinguishes each person from others in the same family and among families.

Aunty and *uncle* are polite forms of address used often by children for any adult who is not a relation. Even vendors at a market stall may use it to communicate with a customer they do not know.

COSTUME

With a few exceptions, Singaporeans wear Western-style dress when they are at work. Other everyday clothes tend to be Eastern or Western depending on how traditional the wearer prefers to be.

Traditional dress is worn only on special occasions. The Chinese cheongsam is still worn during the Chinese New Year and on formal occasions but is otherwise rarely seen.

Malay women still wear the traditional *baju kurung* (bah-joo koo-rohng), a long-sleeve loose blouse worn over an ankle-length skirt known as a sarong. Indians dress in traditional costume mainly for social occasions such as weddings and when going to the temple. The sari, 6 yards (2 m) of material attractively draped around the body, is most commonly worn by women. Men are less likely to be seen in their traditional clothes except at their own weddings or for festive occasions.

Colorful traditional Malay clothes, *kebayas*, on sale in a shop.

IMPORTANCE OF GOLD

Gold is highly valued by each of the ethnic groups for both social and financial reasons. As a precious metal, it is considered a worthwhile investment because of its stable property. For the Chinese, gold jewelry is a special gift for parents to give their daughter when she gets married, a way of wishing her a good marriage and a prosperous life.

Malays buy gold as an investment and for luck. Its importance is seen in the bunga mas (boong-ah mahs), a golden tree that forms one of the ritual aspects of a Malay wedding. It used to be made of real gold, but now gold-colored foil is used instead.

Among Indians, even babies will own a simple gold chain or anklet, and every girl has gold bangles, a gift from her parents that she will wear when she is married.

INTERNET LINKS

http://peranakan.org.sg/home/

Learn more about Peranakan customs and traditions through this website devoted to all things Baba and Nonya.

http://library.thinkquest.org/26477/spore4.htm

This article raises questions about issues of multiculturalism in Singapore.

www.eurasians.org.sg/about/eurasians-in-singapore/

This article examines who the Eurasians are. This Web site is a means through which members of the Eurasian community are able to connect with one another.

LIFESTYLE

A Singaporean family enjoying a sunny
afternoon in front of the Singapore River.

A FTER DECADES OF STRUGGLE, Singaporeans now see themselves as a cosmopolitan people in touch with new ideas and technologies, well on their way to forging a "city of excellence."

To some extent success is taken for granted and the constraints of the past forgotten. The modern nation has shaped a new forward-looking society that still preserves its traditional values.

The Chinese, Malay, and Indian cultures may seem very different, but they share similar values. The Chinese belief in Confucianism, the Malay *adat* (ah-daht), or rules for living, and Indian traditions place loyalty

An Indian family walking along a street in Little India.

Family is the cornerstone of Singaporean society. However, Singapore's birthrate has been experiencing a downward trend, and the government has been trying to reverse this with a series of campaigns and incentives to have children, and even setting up a government agency to match up singles!

to the family and the nation above all else. The government is anxious to emphasize such commonalities so that Singaporeans do not see themselves as disparate races.

SOCIAL INTERACTION

Community spirit is considered very important and is fostered by residents' committees in public housing estates, also known as the "heartlands," where 80 percent of Singaporeans live. The committees arrange a wide range of activities and services and involve themselves in community projects. The goal is to foster racial harmony among the residents of different backgrounds.

The post-World War II baby boom caused a rise in the number of aging citizens for whom services will be required in the near future. With this in mind, the Senior Citizens' Care Services was developed to provide health care as well as recreational activities to help keep this generation active in their community.

Retirees playing checkers at the void deck of a public housing block. The void deck serves as a meeting point for residents, enabling them to bond over activities such as checkers, thus fostering a sense of community.

CIVIL DEFENSE

The aim of the Civil Defence Plan is to prepare as many people as possible for a national crisis. Thousands of trained volunteers form closely knit units that conduct emergency exercises such as food, water, and fuel distribution, or blood grouping and collection. This is done in every constituency at regular intervals to familiarize people with emergency plans and procedures.

The program brings everyone who is not eligible for national military service—youths, women, and senior citizens—to a better understanding of the need for readiness in peacetime. Various means are used: talks, mobile exhibitions, films, posters, competitions, and staging of mock events.

Every year on February 15, the government launches its Total Defence Campaign to remind each citizen of his or her role in defending the nation. The date is symbolic, as it was on February 15, 1942, that Singapore surrendered to the Japanese. Civil defense is just one of five aspects—the others being psychological, social, economic, and military defense—introduced in 1984 to make up the Total Defence Campaign.

FAMILY

More than 80 percent of Singaporeans live in HDB flats, high-rise apartments in public housing estates managed by the HDB. A small minority live in private condominiums and houses.

The resettlement of the population from their traditional lifestyle in the city and coastal areas to the new towns caused a very important social change: the breakup of the extended family. There is no longer the space for grandparents, parents, children, and other relatives to live together. In the 1990s about 85 percent of families in Singapore were families consisting of parents and children only, and the figure today is higher still.

Central to the preservation of the traditional family is filial piety, the lifelong obligation of children to their parents above everyone else. In the past this entailed total obedience; it has now been simplified by some to mean their duty to return the investment made in them.

Other social and economic changes are rapidly taking their toll on the family. An increase in divorce and career involvement and a fall in the birthrate are major concerns that have created a need for counseling services for families having problems. Meanwhile advertising campaigns have been launched emphasizing the more attractive aspects of family life, and in an attempt to encourage couples to have more children, the government offers attractive tax rebates.

CHILDREN

Children are at the center of many Singaporean families. Modern ideas of education and parenting may account for the extra attention Singaporean children are given. Ballet and piano lessons after school, at one time out of the financial reach of most parents, are now common.

Once grandparents were very important caretakers who would tell children stories and pass on values in this way. But now families live in

An extended family, with all their children in tow, dressed in their best during a Muslim festival.

different housing developments, grandparents often work as well as parents, and children spend less time with relatives. Neighbors may look after the children occasionally. As more women join the workforce, parents are using child-care centers or making arrangements with a "nanny," usually a woman living nearby, who will mind the children during the workday for a fee. Many Singaporean families now employ the services of a live-in maid or foreign domestic worker, from the poorer neighboring countries of Indonesia and the Philippines, whose responsibilities include looking after both the home and the children.

Schools are very exam oriented, and there is a lot of pressure on children to study hard and do well. Even at the primary level, there are regular tests, as well as midyear and year-end examinations to keep standards high. After six to eight years of primary school, students move on to secondary school, where they spend four or five years, depending on their ability. Successful secondary school students can then go on to a two-year or three-year preuniversity course as preparation for university study. Others leave and go to technical colleges for vocational training.

Schoolchildren get the chance to observe a hawksbill turtle firsthand. There is a very heavy emphasis on education in Singapore, but schools continually try to find ways to make lessons more exciting and alive.

WOMEN

After the country's independence, free education up to the secondary level for girls as well as boys was coupled with the need for a larger educated workforce. Women were not only able but actively encouraged to make the best use of their education because it was their parents' investment in future prosperity. At the same time, they were expected to fulfill the traditional role of wife and mother. The modern age has presented women with the challenge of managing both, rather than encouraging a choice between one or the other.

Their dilemma is made worse by government pressure on women to marry and have children early as well as contribute to the workforce. Many financially independent women enjoy their working life and are in no hurry to marry. For many of them, busy careers present few opportunities to meet people socially. To encourage more women to marry early and give birth to more children, the government is offering tax incentives to young parents

Children reading books at a child-care center. As more mothers return to work, there has been an increase in demand for child-care services in the country.

and couples with more than two children. In addition, many child-care centers are being set up to enable mothers to return to the workforce while having peace of mind that their children are well taken care of during the day.

BIRTH

A dramatic fall in the birthrate in the late 1980s changed the family-planning policy of "Girl or Boy—Two Is Enough" to "Have Three or More If You Can Afford It." Almost overnight, advertisers and government departments had to switch from making larger families seem unattractive to making them seem a normal aspect of life. Illustrations in school textbooks were revised to conform to the change in government policy, and television no longer ran advertisements showing mothers being worn down by screaming children.

As of 2010, the birthrate in Singapore was 8.65 births per 1,000 people. In 2004 a package of measures was introduced to address the declining birthrate and support parenthood, which included financial incentives and

Most families in Singapore were encouraged to have only two children—a trend that the government is now trying to reverse due to the falling birthrate.

nonfinancial benefits. The package includes the Parenthood Tax Rebate, which offers parents S$5,000 (US$3,859) for the first child, S$10,000 (US$7,718) for the second child, and S$20,000 (US$15,437) for the third child and any subsequent children. Another financial incentive is the working mothers' child relief, which offers working mothers a reward of up to 25 percent of their earnings, depending on the number of children they have. Other benefits offered include longer maternity leave of 12 weeks paid leave, child-care leave, infant-care subsidy, foreign domestic worker levy concession, and grandparent caregiver tax relief.

Regardless of government incentives, the fertility rate remains low at 1.22 children per woman. In spite of this, birth has always been a very important social event in Singapore. This is especially true when a boy is born. Asians traditionally believed that they needed a son to carry on the family name or business and to take care of them when they are old. Though women in Singapore have more freedom than in many other Asian societies, the delight a male child brings is still deeply ingrained.

Children having fun playing in fake snow. The fertility rate in Singapore has continued on a downward trend over the years.

ETHNIC PRACTICES REGARDING BIRTH

Nonreligious beliefs and superstitions are common. The new mother is expected to observe certain taboos such as avoiding foods that sap vitality. For at least a month after her baby is born, she is considered "unclean" and must rest at home. During this time she is richly pampered with special foods and tonics to build up her strength.

One month (according to the lunar calendar) after a Chinese baby is born, his or her family will have a celebration. The baby, usually dressed in the lucky color red, is shown off to relatives, while red-colored hard-boiled eggs are distributed as symbols of life and energy. Horoscopes may be consulted for a name that will identify the child as having been born in a certain year or generation.

After a Malay baby's first bath, his or her father recites a Muslim prayer call into the baby's ear to make sure the child grows up a good Muslim. A ritual shaving of the baby's hair is done a week later, after which a feast is held, and the baby is given a name from the Koran.

For the Hindus, a priest chooses the first letter of the baby's name, and on the 28th day after the baby's birth (a lunar month) the child's head is shaved as a thanksgiving. Baby girls may also have their ears pierced at this time.

Ethnic customs regarding birth vary, and among members of the same ethnic group, practices may vary depending on how traditional the family is. Many young families are beginning to break away from elaborate rituals that they consider too expensive or impractical, but a celebratory feast or symbolic prayer ritual at the very least is still common.

PUBERTY

There is little in the way of rites of passage for Singaporeans, as traditional "growing up" ceremonies are not always observed. Malay boys are still circumcised at or before puberty, while some Indians have puberty celebrations for girls to wish them a happy married life in the future. The Chinese do not have puberty rituals in their culture.

For all Singaporean boys, National Service is their acceptance into manhood. Since 1967 all male citizens aged 18 or older have been expected to serve three years of full-time National Service. Most go into the armed forces, but some join the police or the Civil Defence Force. After this, they become reservists, who form 80 percent of the army. Reservists may be called up at any time, so they must sharpen their skills during compulsory in-camp training each year. Singaporean girls do not have to serve.

Singapore has found that a civilian army is a useful and less expensive way of maintaining an adequate defense force. The training also plays an important part in the mental and physical maturation of young Singaporean men. The bonds they form with colleagues of different social and cultural backgrounds and the military skills they learn equip them to be better workers in civilian life.

Recruits serving their National Service going through arms drills on Pulau Tekong, a military training island just off the mainland of Singapore.

Young men and women enjoy spending study or leisure time together. They meet in groups in shopping centers and fast-food restaurants. A generation ago adults would have been scandalized to see young men and women together unchaperoned. Today it is common to see couples spending time together, hand in hand.

Dating in the Western sense is fairly common. Young people have been influenced by the mass media and especially by the notion of romantic love, which sometimes conflicts with the more conservative values of their society.

Peer-group pressure is especially strong with the rise of popular culture. Most teenagers are provided with pocket money, and they might earn additional money by working in fast-food restaurants and shopping centers or by tutoring during school vacations. This results in young people with the spending power of adults without adult expenses, giving rise to fears of a pampered materialistic generation with unrealistic expectations for the future.

A young man chivalrously offers assistance to his date as they rollerblade along East Coast Park.

MARRIAGE AND DIVORCE

Arranged marriages are not as common as they once were, but they still exist, particularly among the Indians and the Malays, who may call upon the traditional services of a matchmaker. Her role is not as extensive as it was in the past, but the matchmaker may pass on information about a potential bride or groom and arrange meetings between families. However, young people often prefer to choose their future spouses.

The usual practice for a wedding in Singapore is for couples to take part in a civil ceremony at the Registry of Marriages. This is essential if they are to be eligible for a public-housing apartment, even though it could be several years before they get the one they want. Until that time, most couples live apart. Religious rites and family celebrations are postponed until the apartment is acquired and furnished and enough money is saved for a customary marriage celebration.

The Chinese may observe their traditional tea ceremony. As a sign of respect to their family elders, newlyweds serve them tea in order of seniority.

A traditional Hindu wedding at the Sri Srinivasa Perumal Temple.

GOVERNMENT MATCHMAKERS

The Social Development Unit (SDU) is a government agency that works with private companies to offer a modern matchmaking service that encourages male and female graduates to meet, enjoy each other's company during arranged activities, and hopefully consider marriage. In this government-run project, the emphasis is not just on marriage but on marriages between people of equal education. A second, related project is the formation of Social Development Clubs. These have been set up throughout Singapore to organize activities among single nongraduates for the same purpose. These ideas took some time to be accepted, but the formation of the SDU in 1985 has led to the happy marriages of 33,000 of its members.

The tea ceremony is almost always followed by a lavish feast in the evening, where friends and family gather to celebrate the marriage.

While the rituals take different forms, the Western white wedding dress is a popular choice. On Sundays and public holidays, parks are turned into open-air photography studios where local brides parade in the latest bridal fashions.

Malays are married under Muslim law with a traditionally elaborate one-day ceremony. This is usually a very public affair announced by a pair of poles topped with sprays of colored paper twisted around wooden spikes. Called the *bunga manggar* (boong-eh mahng-gahr), this depicts a mango tree in bloom to wish the couple many children. The couple do not live together until after the *bersanding* (ber-sahn-ding), when the bride and the groom are placed on a raised platform in front of the guests and treated as queen and king. Everyone then joins in a *kenduri* (ken-doo-ree), or celebratory feast.

Hindu wedding ceremonies are a series of symbolic rituals carried out in a temple. The most significant is when the groom ties the *thali* (tha-lee), a gold pendant, around the bride's neck to symbolize their marriage. Traditional dowries are still paid, although these are not as large as in the past.

Interracial marriages are not uncommon, because many couples think of themselves as Singaporeans rather than belonging to a particular race.

Divorce in Singapore is on the rise—more than 7 percent in 2010—mainly among the Chinese, followed by the Malays. It is low among Indians because the role of a married person is very important in their culture and gives the women status among friends and relatives.

Muslims are governed by Islamic, or shariah, law in matters such as marriage and divorce. A Muslim woman can ask to divorce her husband if he fails to support her or treats her badly; a Muslim man is allowed up to four wives at a time. Marriage by Singapore law is monogamous for non-Muslims, however, unlike in the past when Chinese men could have several wives.

DEATH

Most aspects of life in Singapore have been modernized. Funerals are no exception. At some Chinese funerals, it is not unusual to see the dead person in Western-style dress instead of layers of clothes specially prepared for the

Memorial niches with offerings to the deceased at the Kong Meng San Phor Kark See Monastery.

occasion. Western bands often take the place of the more somber Chinese musicians, and elaborately decorated truck-hearses are being replaced by glass-sided hearses. These are little more than outward differences because the religious beliefs behind the old rituals remain unchanged. Mourning still lasts the customary 49 days, by which time the dead person is believed to have been reincarnated. The complexity of the rituals varies according to a family's financial situation and preferences, but even the simplest funeral is generally expensive. After the ritual, the body is either buried or cremated and the ashes placed in an urn in a columbarium.

Muslim religious beliefs do not allow for cremation. A pair of vertical stones at the head and foot of the grave are embedded in soil or cemented onto slabs. Rounded headstones are used for men and flat ones for women. Muslims believe they will be reunited with Allah (God), whereas Hindus believe they will be reborn to make amends for their past sins. For Hindus, the funeral ceremony is usually held at home, after which the body is cremated at a crematorium and the ashes thrown into the sea.

INTERNET LINKS

www.lovebyte.org.sg/web/ent_p_home.asp

The official website of the Social Development Unit, a government agency set up to help single Singaporeans find life partners.

http://iprep.ns.sg/

A website set up to help boys about to enlist in National Service. It contains information on what to expect as well as how to prepare for National Service.

www.family.org.sg/Default.aspx?cat=0

A local organization that runs programs and events aimed at helping Singaporean families thrive.

RELIGION

Intricate carvings and details on the Sri Srinivasa Perumal Temple in Little India in Singapore.

8

SINGAPORE IS A SECULAR STATE where freedom of worship is offered to everyone. Religion and race are closely bound, and people of different faiths respect and tolerate each other's beliefs.

According to the 2000 census, 42.5 percent of the population is Buddhist, 14.9 percent Muslim, 8.5 percent Taoist, 4 percent Hindu, 4.8 percent Catholic, 9.8 percent belong to other Christian groups and 0.6 percent to other religions, and 14.8 percent of Singaporeans have no religious beliefs.

MAIN RELIGIONS

TAOISM When Chinese immigrants first came to Singapore in the 19th century, Chinese Buddhism had absorbed many Taoist beliefs and customs. The distinction between the two philosophies became blurred, and many people practiced varying combinations of the two.

Taoism is a very old belief system. It began with the teachings of Lao-tzu, a Chinese sage who believed in Tao (the Way), a path by which people could live in harmony with nature. Centuries later it began to be associated with geomancy (divination by geographic features or numbers), astrology,

Right: Devotees praying at the Thian Hock Keng Temple in Singapore.

79

Muslim men at their Friday prayers at the Abdul Gaffoor Mosque.

and magic and later with Confucian ethics. Its followers in Singapore are mainly the older and less educated Chinese who continue to practice these folk beliefs as a way of maintaining old traditions.

BUDDHISM This religion stems from the philosophy of Buddha, an Indian prince who gave up a life of luxury to search for a way to transcend suffering. After years of sacrifice he was "enlightened" and achieved perfect wisdom. This is said to be possible only by following various "noble" paths with the aim of eliminating all human desires.

Most Singaporean Buddhists are Chinese and follow the Mahayana tradition of Buddhism, where merit is gained through good works. The smaller, more monastic Theravada tradition practiced in Sri Lanka and Thailand also has established temples in Singapore. The two traditions have been brought closer together by programs to promote Buddhism through literature, public talks, and classes as well as social services.

ISLAM Islam was brought to Southeast Asia in the 12th century by Indian and Arab traders. The founder of Islam was the prophet Muhammad, and his followers are called Muslims. They believe in one God, Allah, and follow a set of beliefs referred to as the Five Pillars of Wisdom, which are laid out in their holy book, the Koran.

Almost all Singaporean Malays are Muslims, as are some Indians and Chinese. Religious practice is very much a part of their private and social lives, and they are reminded of their duties daily by a call to prayer, broadcast over the radio or from the mosque, the Muslim place of worship. Muslims are supposed to pray five times a day—before sunrise, in the early and late afternoon, after sunset, and before going to bed.

HINDUISM This is a religion that reasons that all faiths are simply different paths to the same God. A Hindu believes that living things have souls that are

CONFUCIUS AND HIS PHILOSOPHY OF LIFE

Kung Fu-tzu was a learned man who held a high position in the Chinese court in the fifth century. He became known as Confucius when a Jesuit priest in China translated his name as such into Latin. His philosophy, Confucianism, is a system of moral ethics. Along with the main religions, including Buddhism and Taoism, it formed the basis of society, education, and administration in China until the 20th century.

In a migrant society like Singapore, Confucianism remains popular with the Chinese because it stresses the importance of keeping ancient traditions alive.

reincarnated or reborn after death and that people's conduct in the present will have a direct effect on what becomes of them in the future. Almost all Hindus in Singapore are Indian.

The Indians, like the other ethnic groups, brought their religion with them and built temples on various parts of the island. Hinduism once pervaded all Southeast Asia but lost its hold, since unlike Islam it is not a missionary religion. Singaporean Hindus, perhaps because they are a minority, are a devout group and even maintain some religious customs that have almost died out in India.

CHRISTIANITY There are a growing number of Christians in Singapore. The percentage of Protestants is growing faster than that of Catholics. More than half of these Christians are converts, mainly English-educated Chinese. The growth in Christianity is attributed to a dissatisfaction with traditional religions and a search for an alternative that is believed to be more modern and rational.

PLACES OF WORSHIP

Early Chinese and Indian temples are among the oldest buildings in Singapore, with some being preserved as national monuments.

Orchard Road Presbyterian Church was first built in 1878 and still hosts services today.

In Chinese temples deities are displayed in niches or on altars, with the most important deity in the center. Hindu temples are always dedicated to one of the Hindu trinity—the gods of creation, preservation, and destruction—who can be worshiped through any of a number of attendant deities.

Muslims must pray five times a day wherever they are and do not worship any images at all. In the mosque, prayers are held under the direction of a religious leader, the imam. Groups of men meet for daily prayers and special rituals, but women worshipers are not permitted to mix with them. In the evenings, the mosque is used to teach children to read the Koran. Mosques are full of worshipers on Friday, the most important day of the week for Muslims.

With the growth in Christianity there has been a parallel growth in Christian churches, with some groups taking over buildings erected for other purposes and turning them into places of worship.

HOLY SYMBOLS

Abstract thought is often represented by symbols. The main religions of Singapore have symbols that convey their special philosophy or doctrine.

THE EIGHT TRIGRAMS Originating from one of the oldest Chinese texts, the I Ching, these are an arrangement of occult signs consisting of combinations of straight lines within a circle. The continuous line is a male symbol, or yang principle, and the broken line is a female symbol, or yin principle. The pattern in the center represents harmony in the universe, a perfect balance between yin and yang. A plaque engraved or painted with the eight trigrams is considered to have the power to protect a home from misfortune and can often be seen hanging over doorways.

TEMPLE AND MOSQUE ARCHITECTURE

Chinese temples are arranged in a series of squares with the central one housing the main temple god. They usually face south on elevated ground, according to strict geomantic rules. Huge wooden beams and elaborately decorated pillars support the roof, which usually tilts upward at each end. This is decorated with glazed tiles supporting porcelain gods and symbolic creatures such as the dragon, which is believed to bring luck, longevity, or wisdom.

There is no set pattern to the way Hindu temples are built. Most have shrines containing deities, with the main shrine facing east in line with the open door; a hall for worshipers; and an elaborately decorated tower called a gopuram. *This used to be for distant pilgrims to pray to when they could not go to the temple.*

Mosques range from the traditional to the ultramodern. All of them have large courtyards where worshipers can prostrate themselves; an area for ritual washing before prayer; and a minaret, a tower from which loudspeakers call Muslims to prayer. Mosques are decorated with carved geometric designs and plant motifs as well as Arabic calligraphy, an essential part of Islamic art.

OM The words and syllables of the holy Vedas, ancient Indian scriptures, have always been revered by Hindus, and certain syllables are believed to be particularly holy. The word om is said to contain the essence of the Vedas, giving it power and mystery. Among the Hindu Brahmins, the priestly sect, om symbolizes the entire universe. It is repeated during worship and as a sacred utterance during meditation.

THE BODHI TREE This is an important Buddhist symbol because Buddhists believe that while sitting under this large fig tree the Buddha attained enlightenment. *Bodhi* (boh-dhee) is an Indian term that means "awakening." Saplings grown in various monasteries are said to be descended from the original tree under which Buddha sat and are therefore treated as sacred. In Singapore there is a bodhi tree outside the Sri Lankaramaya Buddhist Temple's main prayer hall. The tree arrived as a sapling from Sri Lanka.

FOLK BELIEFS

The elderly and less educated Chinese are heavily influenced by the supernatural and believe in appeasing ghosts and ancestors or consulting mediums, people believed to possess the power to communicate with the dead.

The once-powerful Malay *bomoh* (boh-moh), part healer, part adviser, is believed to be in touch with the spirit world. He offers his services in exorcism or matchmaking for a small donation. Like the Indian medicine man and the traditional Chinese doctor, or *sinseh* (sin-sayh), he uses herbs to cure. If these do not work, the *bomoh* relies on magic and incantation.

According to traditional Chinese medicine, illness is caused by a loss of inner, or yin/yang, balance in the body that can be restored by various herbal remedies. This corresponds with the Indian system known as ayurveda, where illness is said to be caused by an imbalance of body fluids. The Malays have a similar faith in *jamu* (jah-moo), an herbal mixture that is ground and then drunk as a panacea for a variety of ills. Traditional medicine is an alternative to Western medicine because it is inexpensive, and research has shown much of it to be reliable—the main difference is that it treats the whole body and not just the part that is symptomatic.

FENG SHUI Modern belief in feng shui combines beliefs in yin and yang, ghosts, and ancestor worship. It also asserts that natural objects and the universe have souls. The practice is a set of rules that allow people to live in harmony with nature. It is a system that provides guidelines for placing buildings and graves in their most favorable positions, and it is taken seriously even in modern Singapore.

NUMEROLOGY Many Singaporeans, in particular those from the Chinese community, believe in the power of numbers and practice a form of numerology. Numerology is based on a complex system whereby the numbers from one's date of birth are combined using various permutations

A statue of Lord Ganesh at Sri Mariamman Temple. The swastika, painted on Lord Ganesh's face above, is a symbol of auspiciousness to Hindus.

THE YIN-YANG PRINCIPLE

The Chinese believe that the world is made up of chi, or creative energy, which is responsible for yin and yang. These are idealized opposites that dominate nature yet remain unnoticed within it, blending with each other in constantly changing amounts. Heaven is yang, Earth is yin, and everything in the universe is contained in these basic forces. Yang is positive, active, masculine, and found in everything warm, dry, and bright. Yin is negative, passive, feminine, and found in things soft, shady, and secret.

The Chinese strive to balance these two states to create harmony in their lives. Too much of either creates an imbalance that must be corrected if one is to live happily. This principle is even applied to eating and to illness, since the yin/yang balance is believed to affect the human body from both inside and outside.

to predict the outcome of one's future or to uncover one's personality type. Singaporeans use numerology when deciding which day to get married, whether to buy a property, and even which job to take. According to Chinese numerology, 4 is a very unlucky number, as it sounds like the word for death in the Cantonese dialect. The number 8, however, is extremely lucky, as it sounds like the word for wealth. It is no coincidence that the opening ceremony of China's 2008 Olympics was held on the eighth day of the eighth month (August 8, 2008)—considered a most auspicious day.

INTERNET LINKS

http://countrystudies.us/singapore/24.htm

A succinct overview about religion in Singapore and the different beliefs that each ethnic group adheres to.

http://weecheng.com/singapore/tanki/

A website devoted to the beliefs and practices of folk Taoism. The site covers festivals, and includes images and links.

LANGUAGE

A man passes some time reading the newspaper.

THERE ARE FOUR OFFICIAL languages: Malay, the national language; Mandarin, the official language used by the majority Chinese group; Tamil, the language of more than half of Singapore's Indians; and English, the language of business and administration, which blends these cultures together.

Most Singaporeans are multilingual, but each individual speaks a primary language. According to the 2000 census, 35 percent of the population speak Mandarin as their primary language, 23 percent speak English, and 14 percent speak Malay. Among the main Chinese dialects, 11.4 percent speak Hokkien, 5.7 percent speak Cantonese, 4.9 percent speak Teochew, another 3.2 percent speak the Indian language of Tamil, and 1.8 percent speak other Chinese dialects.

Singapore's literacy rate is 92.5 percent. The literacy rate among men is 96.6 percent, whereas among women it is 88.6 percent.

A DIVERSITY OF TONGUES

Most people in Singapore speak at least one of the local languages and English. Each ethnic majority is encouraged to continue using its mother tongue, which is a very

Right: A man on the telephone in Tekka Market in Little India.

9

Most Singaporeans are able to speak another language besides English. Singapore's multilingual culture has given rise to Singlish, a mishmash of English, Malay, Mandarin, and other Chinese dialects.

Two office workers catching up over their lunch break at Raffles Place.

important vehicle for the transmission of beliefs and values to the next generation.

Although English is often spoken well, a local variation is also used. This is referred to as "Singlish," an amalgam of English, various Chinese dialects, and Malay. It is not grammatical and is spoken with a singsong accent, the voice lifting at the end of groups of words.

NONVERBAL LANGUAGE

Thoughts and feelings remain largely unsaid in Singapore, especially among the older generation, so an intermediary object or person may be used to convey nonverbal messages. For example, an old Chinese couple may show concern for each other through their grandchild by saying, "Tell your grandma to take a rest." The younger generation, however, is generally more outspoken and expressive.

One important facet of unexpressed emotion is "loss of face," a sensation of inferiority or humiliation as a result of feeling "exposed" in front of others. A child will not argue with his or her parents in public for fear of embarrassing his or her family, and a worker does not question his or her superiors in case he or she appears to question their judgment. Thus out of politeness and to save face, a Singaporean may publicly agree to do something that privately he or she does not intend to do.

Singaporeans may laugh at situations that do not seem funny to a Westerner, and therefore, it is important to distinguish between laughter and humor. Laughter is sometimes a cover for embarrassment, to hide loss of face.

Some gestures are shared by all ethnic groups. Handshakes are the most common form of greeting across cultures, particularly between men and women, although each group has its own style of greeting.

SINGLISH

The multiculturalism of Singapore has produced a unique language that most Singaporeans use on an everyday basis. It is affectionately known as Singlish and is a mixture of British English blended with Malay, Chinese, and words from the Indian languages. Here are some common examples:

Lah

Used at the end of sentences for emphasis.
Example: The shops are closing in five minutes! Go now lah!

Chope

Derived from the English word chop, *it means "to reserve."*
Example: Let's go to the concert early so we can chope *the best seats.*

Kiasu

Originating from the Hokkien dialect, it means "afraid to lose out to others."
Example: He is so kiasu, he will study extra hard to make sure he comes out top in the exams.

Shiok

Originating from the Malay language, it means "great" or "'amazing."
Example: I love the taste of beef noodles—so shiok!

SCRIPT

The Chinese script has remained unchanged for more than a thousand years, the characters standing for a combination of sounds and ideas based on simple pictographs. The addition of extra lines or dots to the pictographs suggests closely related ideas, while two or more pictographs are joined to convey abstract ideas. Pictographic combinations can also suggest two items sharing the same sound. In the 1960s in China, the characters were simplified and standardized, and a few years later Singapore followed suit. Efforts have also been made to standardize the spelling of Chinese words in English by using a system called *hanyu pinyin* (han-yoo pin-yin).

The earliest Malay script was an alphabet of southern Indian origin. Four centuries later Malay was written in an Arabic script called Jawi. Both the Dutch and the British colonialists transcribed the Arabic symbols into the Roman alphabet. The form of Malay used in Singapore has been brought in line with changes made in Malaysia and Indonesia.

The script of the Tamil Indians comes from the oldest Dravidian language, used mainly by people living in Tamil Nadu in southern India and in Sri Lanka. Its basic structure has remained unchanged for almost 2,500 years, yet its script has no connection with other Indian scripts. Tamil was one of the earliest languages to develop a rich store of written literature.

A calligrapher in Chinatown working on some Chinese text.

"SPEAK MANDARIN" CAMPAIGN

In a country as small and diverse as Singapore, similarities rather than differences within groups need to be emphasized. In the 1970s, it was noted that dialects were preventing the Chinese from considering themselves a unified group. So a link among these groups was forged by the adoption of Mandarin, the language of Beijing.

In 1979 a national campaign was mounted, with television advertisements and street slogans, advising citizens to "Speak Mandarin" and not dialects. Mandarin is taught in schools, is used on television and radio, and is now spoken increasingly by Chinese Singaporeans. The older generation still feels more comfortable with dialects, but there are many young Singaporeans who do not understand the language of their ancestors.

INTERNET LINKS

www.goodenglish.org.sg/

Besides the "Speak Mandarin" campaign, Singapore also runs the "Speak Good English Movement," which encourages Singaporean to speak grammatically correct English.

www.singlishdictionary.com/

A dictionary for deciphering Singlish terms.

www.omniglot.com/writing/chinese.htm

A website that takes an in-depth look at the origins of the Chinese script.

ARTS

Members of a dragon dance
troupe pose for the camera.

10

>SINGAPORE HAS THE UNIQUE opportunity to draw upon the rich heritage of its multicultural people. The arts scene takes its inspiration from both East and West. The development of the arts receives support from both private and government institutions.

THEATER AND DRAMA

Cross-cultural influences have added a fresh dimension to well-known works of all ethnic groups.

Chinese street operas have been common in Singapore since the 1940s. Chinese clans and community groups still conduct opera classes and workshops. Performances are usually held during Chinese festivals, and as they are in honor of the gods, they are always free. Today classical Chinese opera can also be enjoyed in air-conditioned theaters with large seating capacities, a reflection of its popularity. Locals and tourists who may not understand the language can enjoy these performances, since there are English subtitles.

Right: A Chinese operatic wooden puppet show in progress.

93

To the Chinese, the lion has been synonymous with scaring demons for centuries. The lion dance did not come to Singapore until 1925, when the first troupe arrived from southern China. The dance was originally associated solely with the Chinese New Year but is now part of any important event. It is accompanied by fierce drumming.

The lion's head with its exaggerated features is a rattan frame decorated in bright colors. It is worn by two men, one crouched behind the other. The impact of the dance, which is intended to show courage, depends on the coordination of these two performers.

The performers are often martial-arts pupils, as the dance is acrobatic and requires much stamina. It takes about a year to learn the steps, but as only skillful dancers are paid for their services, frequent practice is necessary.

The object of the dancers is to overcome various obstacles put in the way and reach some green leaves, usually lettuce—the lion's reward for the good fortune its presence has brought. Originally the cut greens also signified the start of new growth in the fields after the harvest.

Malay theatrical traditions such as *bangsawan* (bung-SAH-one), a type of traditional opera, have seen a revival in recent years as a medium for telling dramatic stories. It is important to note that Malay and Indian drama is rarely complete without music and dance.

Contemporary theater, performed mainly in English to a younger audience, is increasing in popularity. Some drama groups have also started to produce bilingual plays. Established theater companies in Singapore today include Drama Box, The Necessary Stage, Teater Ekamatra, Ravindran Drama Group, and Agni Koothu.

DANCE

The Singapore dance scene consists of both traditional and modern dance companies. The most established group is the Singapore Dance Theatre, but contemporary dance groups such as The Arts Fission Company, Odyssey Dance Theatre, EcNad Project Ltd., and Ah Hock and Peng Yu have started to make their mark.

An example of a popular Chinese traditional dance is the lion dance. Sadly, other traditional Chinese dances are now rarely performed except at cultural shows for tourists.

Malay dance can be divided into two groups: *tarian* (tah-ree-yan), or pure dance, and *taridra* (tah-ree-drah), or dance-drama. Dance steps and moves are learned and memorized so that the dances and their music are not lost. Many cultural groups have been formed to promote Malay dance, and classes are taught at community centers.

Indian dance is considered an important means of keeping the young in touch with their community and religion. However, few young people are happy to spend the many years necessary to learn ancient Indian art forms.

A group of girls preparing to perform an Indian dance.

Launched in 1977, the annual Singapore Arts Festival was established to celebrate the nation's amazing range of art forms from its multiethnic people. The growing success of the festival during the years has helped to make Singapore a vibrant cultural center in the region. It has equally contributed to the growing interest and appreciation of the arts among Singaporeans. There is a wide range of performances and activities for all age groups, from Cantonese opera to street dance. The majority of the performances, however, have a unique Asian influence.

This is especially true of the exacting movements of the Bharathanatyam, a traditional southern Indian devotional dance.

MUSIC

Singaporeans, especially the younger generation, enjoy contemporary Western and Asian pop music. However, traditional ethnic music continues to be appreciated by many as well.

Concerts of the Chinese classics are primarily renditions by the *er hu* (err-hoo) and the *gao hu* (kow-hoo), both stringed instruments, while other small performing groups offer Chinese choral singing and folk songs.

Groups singing traditional love songs called *ghazal* (ghah-zahl) used to be an important part of local Malay wedding entertainment in the 1950s and 1960s. A few of these groups remain, but they now double as wedding bands playing contemporary music. Another form of song is *dikir barat* (dee-kir bah-raht), the choral singing that usually accompanies Malay drama.

Indian music has similar instrumental and vocal traditions, both still heavily influenced by classical forms. In Singapore there are various arts organizations that bring teachers in from India to teach classical music, and performances of both northern and southern Indian music are held onstage.

The Singapore Symphony Orchestra was formed in 1979. Since then it has brought music from baroque to 20th-century composers, including regional works, to the local population.

Besides regular concerts, there is also the annual Festival of Music. During the two-month festival more than 100 groups, both local and foreign, offer a wide variety of music, from jazz and computer music to Chinese, Malay, and Indian traditional music. Some of the performances are held in the open air to bring the music to as many people as possible.

ART AND ARTIFACTS

Among the museums in Singapore are the Singapore Art Museum, the Asian Civilisations Museum, and

The lotus-shaped ArtScience Museum.

the Singapore History Museum, which help preserve and present the cultural heritage of Singaporeans through their acquisitions and exhibitions.

The collection of the Singapore Art Museum has been built from a gift of some early local works by a local philanthropist in the 1960s. In recent years the museum has acquired a strong collection of art by local and Southeast Asian artists and has moved into a heritage building that used to be a school in the heart of Singapore's cultural district.

The Asian Civilisations Museum is in the former Empress Place Building, which once housed government offices. The museum's collection includes Asian stone sculptures, traditional textiles, ceramics, and other ancient objects.

Exhibitions detailing the history of Singapore are the focus of the History Museum, which also organizes educational shows featuring the foods and handicrafts of the various ethnic cultures in the region.

Many Singaporean artists taught at the republic's premier art school, the Nanyang Academy of Fine Arts, set up in 1938. Famous Singaporean artists include Cheong Soo Pieng, Chen Chong Swee, Georgette Chen, Chen Wen Hsi, and Liu Kang. These artists created their own style of painting, which combined contemporary Western ideas with ancient Eastern methods.

The newest of Singapore's museums, the ArtScience Museum in Marina Bay, opened in 2011. It is housed in a unique lotus-shaped building and includes more than 5,502 square yards (4,600 square m) of gallery space.

Singapore's skyline is dominated by the Esplanade—an architecturally interesting structure built in the shape of two giant shells. Locals have likened its unique shape to that of a well-loved local fruit, the durian. Opened in 2002 and located at the mouth of the historic Singapore River, the Esplanade is the republic's premier arts center. All forms of art are catered for at this venue including music, dance, theater, and the visual arts. There are five auditoriums including a concert hall and an opera-house-style theater that can accommodate 3,600 attendees. There are also several outdoor performance spaces and a mix of offices, shops, restaurants, and apartments. With its superb facilities and services, the Esplanade has attracted renowned artists from all over the world.

LITERATURE

Singapore has a very high literacy rate, and Singaporeans enjoy reading for information and pleasure. Great numbers of people regularly fill the aisles of local bookshops and libraries.

There is a growing interest in local literature—written in all four official languages—and an increasing number of published Singaporean writers. Well-known local writers include Catherine Lim, Edwin Thumboo, Wong Meng Voon, Abdul Ghani Bin Abdul Hamid, and Rama Kannabiran. Books dealing with Singaporean subjects appeal to Singaporeans. The development of local literature reflects a consciousness of national identity, as local writers search for a style of their own. The National Book Development Council of Singapore (NBDCS) and the biennial Singapore Writers Festival help promote literary activities in Singapore.

ISKANDAR JALIL, MODERN POTTER

Born in 1939, Iskandar Jalil is a highly regarded artist who has been a potter since 1960. He has made significant contributions to the arts in Singapore, particularly to its modern ceramics history. His innovative designs, based on Japanese styles and influenced by Islamic calligraphy, have been featured in many exhibitions. He uses local materials and retains the earthy quality of the clay rather than rely on glazes. His work is recognizable by his signature "Iskandar blue," luxurious tactile surfaces, and the inclusion of twigs.

Iskandar sees himself more as a craftsman than an artist. In spite of this, he was given a special award for art by the Ministry of Culture in 1975 and awarded the National Cultural Medallion, the highest award in Singapore for the arts, in 1988. In 1998 he was awarded the Pingkat Apad by the Singapore Malay Arts Society, and in 2002 he was awarded the Berita Harian Achiever of the Year award. He enjoys teaching at his own workshop and at local educational establishments, aiming to give his students a strong base in pottery and to leave something of himself behind.

INTERNET LINKS

www.marinabaysands.com/ArtScienceMuseum/

The ArtScience Museum is the newest museum in Singapore. The architecture of the museum was inspired by the lotus flower.

www.nac.gov.sg/

The official website for Singapore's National Arts Council. Take a look at the initiatives that the government supports to boost Singapore's local arts scene.

http://infopedia.nl.sg/articles/SIP_267_2005-01-13.html

An article that examines the life and works of potter Iskandar Jalil.

LEISURE

Two Singaporean Chinese men
having a game of Chinese chess.

>**T**HE MANY OFFSHORE ISLANDS of Singapore are ideal for picnics and snorkeling; a few have camping facilities too. Some Singaporeans like to sunbathe, but most prefer to relax in a shady part of the beach.

They swim in artificially sheltered lagoons because the open sea has been polluted by heavy ocean traffic and many areas have a strong undercurrent. Smaller islets and reefs have been merged to provide suitable areas for boating, sailing, scuba diving, sea fishing, and other marine activities.

There are numerous public parks scattered across the island, each having some particular feature of interest. There are city parks, nature parks, community parks, and heritage parks. Certain coastal parks allow bird life to be observed at close range, while others offer fitness courses with panoramic views of the sea.

City parks provide a number of leisure activities, whether as modern recreation and performance centers or as rejuvenated historical landmarks. Many have reservoirs or lakes and attractive scenery that offer an escape from the city with quiet walks and bird-singing areas.

Right: A girl canoeing in MacRitchie Reservoir.

101

The east coast of Singapore was the refuge of rich island dwellers who lived in large bungalows overlooking the sea. Land reclamation created the East Coast Parkway, the site of fine seafood restaurants, sea sports, camping, barbecues, cycling, and walks along the seafront.

GAMES

Congkak (chong-kak), a traditional Malay game of chance played by adults and children, is one of the many ethnic games now fast disappearing. It requires a long, narrow wooden board with rounded ends, containing two rows of small indentations, or "holes," in which seeds, pebbles, or similar countable objects are placed. As the game progresses, these gradually accumulate in two larger holes at each end, known as the *congkak* "houses." The person with the most seeds collected there wins.

Gasing (gah-sing), or spinning tops, are traditional toys that Malays and Chinese still play with today. The tops are made of wood in two sizes: a large top threaded with string that causes it to spin and a smaller type that can be spun with the finger and thumb.

Carom (CARE-rehm), a game of Indian origin, is very popular in Singapore. Played by two to four players, it is similar to the American game of pool but is much smaller in scale and does not use cues. It consists of a board about 2 feet (61 cm) square with a net pocket at each corner. Counters are pocketed by means of a colored "striker" flicked with the finger and thumb. The object of the game is to remove as many of the opponents' counters from the board as possible.

Mah-jongg is another game that is extremely popular in Singapore. Played with tiles, it was originally played by the aristocracy in China. These tiles, now made of plastic rather than ivory as in the past, are engraved with sets of Chinese symbols and characters. The object is to complete a winning hand of certain sets of tiles as quickly as possible while preventing opponents from

Singaporeans practicing tai chi at the Botanic Gardens.

CHINESE CHESS

Chinese chess, or xiang qi (see-ang chee), is a game of strategy for more intellectual players. Like Western chess, it has 64 squares on the board, but pieces are placed where the lines cross rather than in the squares. It is also separated into two opposing countries with a "river" in the middle. Each country, or side, has 16 pieces consisting of various military forces.

Another form of chess is wei qi (way-chee), sometimes called Go. In this game, the opponent's pieces are surrounded rather than captured. The game is growing in popularity in community centers because it has few rules yet can be played at many levels of complexity.

doing the same. Neighborhoods come alive with the noise of the clickity-clackity sound of the movement of the tiles during weekend mah-jongg parties and the Chinese New Year.

One of the more modern games played in the school playground is zero point, popular among girls. A series of elastic bands strung together make a long flexible "rope." A child holds each end, while a third makes skillful maneuvers across the bands as they are raised gradually from ankle height to head height. Skateboarding and cycling stunts with BMX bikes are very popular among boys.

SPORTS

Singapore's sports facilities include indoor and outdoor stadiums, tracks, multipurpose playing fields, sports halls, swimming complexes, and a sailing lagoon, as well as outdoor exercise apparatus in public fitness parks. Bicycling is gaining popularity. There are many dedicated cycling areas that allow cyclists to get around, exercise, and see the sights, for example, at the East Coast Parkway.

One traditional sporting game still played is *sepak raga* (say-pahk rah gah). *Sepak* in Malay means "to kick," and *raga* means "basket," referring to

A game of soccer being played at the Padang.

a ball made of woven rattan. The ball, which must not be allowed to touch the ground, is tossed to players of a team using any part of the body but the hands. Until recently, no proper rules existed for the game, but it has now been formalized and is popularly known by its Thai name, *sepak takraw* (say-pak tahk-raw).

Soccer, rugby, cricket, field hockey, and golf were introduced by the British, and soccer is considered to be the national sport. Previously Singapore's national team vied with Malaysian states for the Malaysia Cup. In 1995, however, Singapore pulled out of the competition with Malaysia and set up 12 professional soccer clubs.

Cricket is linked to the Padang, the field in front of the Supreme Court building, where it has been played since the 1820s. The cricket season is from March to September, after which rugby takes over until the following March. Field hockey and tennis are also played on the Padang.

Once considered to be a game for the elderly, golf is now growing in popularity among the island's social elite. It is expensive to play golf in Singapore, as there are no public courses. Golfers must be members of one of the many private golf clubs.

Water sports, especially boating and fishing, are popular activities on the east coast and, more recently, in the newly cleaned rivers. The World Powerboat Grand Prix, the International Water Ski Championships, and the International Dragon Boat Races have been held in Singapore waters.

Tai-chi and qigong have a large following, especially among the elderly. These are forms of martial art, where passive movements build inner vitality, strengthen the body, and rest the mind.

STORYTELLING

Storytelling is a Chinese tradition that developed as a form of theatrical entertainment, but such traditional forms are dying out in Singapore. In the past, fine storytellers, often illiterate, would sit under a tree in Chinatown or at Boat Quay, telling a story in the time it took a joss stick to burn. They would then collect payment from the audience. These men have all grown old now, but the tradition lives on in some clan associations.

Although the storytellers drew on well-known tales, they also told entertaining anecdotes to make the stories more exciting. Their traditional role has now been taken over by storytelling sessions in libraries, which take a more modern slant, complete with accompanying discussions and activities, and to a lesser extent by bookshops and television.

Malays have a great store of folktales told by generations of wandering storytellers. Most of their traditional literature, both prose and poetry, has been kept alive by word of mouth and is an art form widely used to pass on social and moral values.

Sanskrit scripture has passages that use stories for both religious and secular reasons. *Ramayana*, an epic poem about a much-loved Hindu deity, Rama, has unparalleled popularity in Southeast Asia and is told through dance dramas or at festival times.

VACATION PURSUITS

Seaside retreats on the offshore island of Sentosa offering an overnight stay include vacation chalets, hostels for large groups of young people, and campsites with tents, barbecue pits, and camp beds for rent. Those who want to stay closer to home book into chalets along the east coast or even into local hotels for a period of uninterrupted luxury.

On long weekends, trips are often made across the short causeway into Malaysia by bus, car, or train and to the nearby Indonesian islands of Bintan and Batam, which have been developed into resort areas thanks to an infusion of Singapore dollars. Proof of the popularity of Malaysia as a tourist destination lies in the long lines of cars waiting for immigration formalities at both ends of the causeway.

Thirty years ago, visiting places beyond Malaysia was a luxury available only to the rich. Today most people want to travel to see the world and take time off from work to do so. Australia, Europe, China, and the United States are favorite destinations.

HOBBIES AND PASTIMES

Most Singaporeans work a five-day or five-and-a-half-day week, so evenings, and particularly Sundays, are opportunities to unwind and indulge in favorite pastimes. Many of these activities are organized by groups promoting social and recreational events for adults and children. The People's Association, a governmental body established in 1960 to promote racial harmony and social cohesion, oversees a network of community centers throughout the island that offer a changing list of cultural programs, crafts, and skills training.

Karaoke, Japanese for "empty orchestra," is a hobby that took Singapore by storm in the 1980s. Enthusiasts meet at karaoke lounges, where song lyrics and video images of scenery are provided. At some, singers can see themselves on television monitors and a big screen.

Kite flying has been a favorite pastime for centuries and is still common in Singapore. Kites are made from thin, oily paper or cellophane and can be quite elaborate in shape and design. Each year there is a National Kite Flying Festival in which teams from many nations participate.

Windsurfers on the sea off the coast of Singapore.

Other enjoyable pastimes for Singaporeans are two national obsessions: shopping and eating. Singapore has often been referred to as "a shopper's paradise" because of its convenient shopping plazas, long business hours, safety, and duty-free imports. A vast range of commodities means almost anything is available, from a designer coat to the newest electronic gadget.

Eating is a social activity enjoyed by all, although lunching out informally is more common than dining together in the evening. Restaurants are particularly busy during weekends, when the whole family will make this a special trip. Food courts are becoming popular. For people anxious to squeeze in as much pleasure as possible on their days off, these air-conditioned areas in shopping centers serve a range of fast food from sushi to frozen yogurt.

SONGBIRDS

People of all ethnic groups keep untrained songbirds because they are inexpensive and easily cared for in small apartments. Although it was once an interest only for elderly men, training these songbirds has become so popular a hobby in modern Singapore that many coffee shops and housing developments include a bird corner equipped with poles and wires to hang cages. Made out of bamboo, these cages are beautifully carved and decorated with ivory ornaments and porcelain bowls.

The first bird-singing competition was held in 1953, just for pleasure. Now owners go to a lot of trouble to train singing birds, which can win them thousands of dollars in prize money. A National Songbird Competition has been held annually since 1982, but many local competitions organized by community centers are held throughout the year.

During the competitions, hundreds of birdcages are hung from poles out in the open. Birds are judged on the basis of their movements, physique, stamina, and singing times.

INTERNET LINKS

www.sepaktakraw.org/

Learn more about the exciting game of *sepak takraw* or *sepak raga*.

http://storytellingsingapore.com/about

A website aimed at keeping the art of storytelling alive. Storytellers are also able to join the association to practice their storytelling skills.

www.cnngo.com/singapore/play/skateboarding-singapores-serious-extreme-sport-672704

An interesting article about skateboarding in Singapore.

FESTIVALS

Hindu devotees walk across smoldering coals in honor of the goddess Draupadi.

12

>S INGAPORE'S ETHNIC AND RELIGIOUS diversity means that its calendar is filled with festivals, adding more color and life to an already bustling tropical island.

TAOIST/BUDDHIST FESTIVALS

The Dragon Boat Festival is held in remembrance of the death of a famous Chinese poet, Qu Yuan, who in protest against corruption threw himself into the Miluo River in China in 278 B.C. Local fishermen rushed out in their boats to save him, throwing mounds of rice into the water and beating drums to keep hungry fish away. To mark the occasion in Singapore, local and international teams of 22 rowers and a drummer complete a 760-yard (695-m) race in long fiberglass boats decorated like dragons, each painted with scales and sporting an awesome head and sharp tail.

Qingming, also known as Ching Min, is the festival often referred to as the Chinese All Souls' Day and is an important event for a people who do not believe that family relationships are broken by death. In the old agricultural communities of China, the dead were seen as being able to ensure a good harvest. Now they are seen to benefit families who honor their memory.

Right: A shrine with offerings to ghosts during the Festival of the Hungry Ghost in Singapore.

Decorations in the Chinese Gardens during the Mid-Autumn Festival. Children can often be seen carrying lanterns around their neighborhoods during this time.

The Festival of the Hungry Ghosts stems from the belief that for one month each year, the dead return to earth and must be entertained. Because of the mischief these ghosts can cause, there are no marriages, family festivities, or important undertakings during this month.

The Mid-Autumn or Mooncake Festival falls in the month when the moon is said to be at its brightest. Chinese Singaporeans observe it as their ancestors would have, with music, family outings, and mooncakes. These are round golden-brown pastries stuffed with a variety of ingredients including beans, lotus seeds, preserved duck eggs, and nuts.

The Chinese or Lunar New Year is the best-loved Chinese festival. It is also called the Spring Festival because for the agricultural people of China, this was an important time to give thanks for the harvest and pray for the coming year. Today it is a time to review the past and make plans for the future. The reunion dinner on Lunar New Year's Eve is the most important event of the year, and all family members are expected to attend.

In preparation for the new year, household objects may be painted red to attract luck, as red denotes success. Red clothes are worn for the same reason; a red banner over the door brings luck to those who enter the house; and children receive *hongbao* (hong-pao), small red packets containing money, for good luck.

Vesak Day marks Buddha's birth, enlightenment, and death according to the Buddhist lunar calendar and is named after the month it falls in. Buddhists fast on this day, bring flowers and fruit to the temple, listen to the monks chanting, and pray. They are expected to do good deeds ranging from feeding the poor to releasing caged birds.

THE CHINESE LUNAR CALENDAR

Ancient Chinese astrologers invented a calendar based on a 60-year cycle—made up of five 12-year cycles—that is still used today. Each of these 12 years has the name of an animal to make it easy to remember.

Each year is divided into six "large moons" of 30 days and six "small moons" of 29 days, based on the moon's movement around the earth. Because the lunar year has 354 days compared with the 365 1/4 days of the solar calendar, they compensated for the difference by adding an extra month to every third year in the 12-year cycle.

Legend has it that Buddha called the animals to him with the object of pairing each of them with a year in the lunar cycle. The first to arrive was the rat, followed by the ox, the tiger, the rabbit, the dragon, the snake, the horse, the goat, the monkey, the rooster, the dog, and the pig. Thus each cycle begins with the Year of the Rat and ends with the Year of the Pig, and people born in a given year are said to take on characteristics of that year's animal.

MUSLIM FESTIVALS

Hari Raya Puasa, or Hari Raya Idul Fitri, is the biggest celebration of the Muslim calendar. It follows immediately after Ramadan, the month of fasting when Muslims do not eat or drink between sunrise and sunset. Fasting is believed to purify the body and soul and is a reminder of the suffering of others.

During the fasting month, shops and markets turn out cakes, sweets, and pastries. Just before the appearance of the new moon, new clothes are bought, houses are cleaned, and people are busy preparing special food for the festivities. It is also common for families to visit cemeteries to tidy grave sites and recite verses from the Muslim holy book, the Koran.

A customary annual ritual is to ask forgiveness from elders for past misdeeds. Children receive money in green packets rather like the Chinese *hongbao*, and all Muslims must contribute an annual *fitrah* (fit-rah), a tithe

The Muslim era dates from the year in which Muhammad migrated from Mecca to Medina. The first day of the first year was fixed at July 16, 622. The years of the Muslim calendar are lunar and always consist of 12 lunar months alternately 30 and 29 days long. The year usually has 354 days, but the last month sometimes has 30 days, making a total of 355 days for that year.

that is used by the Muslim religious council for several purposes, one of which is to help poor students. It is not a tax but a means of giving to others.

Hari Raya Haji, or Hari Raya Aidil Adha (Great Day of Sacrifice), marks the period of the hajj, or annual pilgrimage to Mecca, which falls during the last month of the Muslim calendar, five weeks after the month-long fasting ends. It is very important for a Muslim to make a trip to the holy city of Mecca at least once in his or her lifetime and join the faithful from other parts of the world.

The trip will earn the male Muslim the title hajj and a woman *hajjah* (hah-jah). Prayers of thanks and ritual animal sacrifices are offered at mosques in memory of the willingness of Ibrahim (Abraham) to sacrifice his own son in obedience to Allah's will.

HINDU FESTIVALS

Navratri, or the Festival of Nine Nights, pays homage to the goddesses Durga (Parvathi), Lakshmi, and Saraswathi, consorts to the Hindu Trinity. Three days of the festival are allotted to each form of the goddess. Each represents a different aspect of God, and any one of them can be worshipped in various personal ways. Their freshly garlanded images are dressed and displayed prominently in temples, offerings are laid before them, and each night performances of classical dance and music are held.

Thaipusam is a festival when male Hindu devotees walk barefoot along a 2-mile (3-km) route carrying a heavy steel framework, or *kavadi* (kah-vah-di),

A Hindu devotee carrying a *kadavi* during Thaipusam. These steel frameworks are anchored directly onto the bodies of devotees.

weighing up to 70 pounds (32 kg). This is anchored onto their bare flesh with small hooks and adorned with limes, images of gods, small vessels of milk, and peacock feathers.

The practice has its beginnings in a story of a devotee in India struggling under a load to reach Lord Shiva's son, Lord Murugan, who had summoned him. Since then, devotees perform this act as penance or in thanks for a wish granted. Women carry a smaller *kavadi* on their shoulders, and their cheeks and tongues are often pierced.

Thimithi honors the Hindu goddess Draupadi. More than a thousand devotees walk, seemingly oblivious to pain, across a 10-foot-long (3-m-long) pit filled with smoldering coal, to give thanks for her help in overcoming problems. In a related ceremony, women devotees circle the temple ground, kneeling in prayer after every third step.

Deepavali, which means "a garland of lights," is also known as the Festival of Lights. The date of this New Year festival is set according to the Hindu

THE MAHABHARATA

This Indian epic poem narrates the struggle for supremacy between two related families, the Kauravas and the Pandavas. In one story, Draupadi is pledged in marriage to the five Pandava brothers, but their jealous cousin Duryodhana challenges the eldest Pandava brother to a game of dice and wins her for himself. When he begins to disrobe her, she is saved from humiliation by Lord Krishna to whom she appeals for help. She curses Duryodhana and swears she will not braid her hair until she can oil it with his blood. When he eventually dies, she performs her grisly task and walks on fire to prove her chastity. Devotees follow her example to prove they have similarly kept an important vow.

Vikrama calendar, and it usually falls in October or November. Deepavali celebrates Lord Krishna's victory over the demon of darkness. In Singapore, electric lights now decorate the streets and houses, taking the place of the traditional oil lamps.

CHRISTIAN FESTIVALS

Good Friday is commemorated with night services in churches to mark the occasion of the crucifixion of Christ. At Saint Joseph's Church, worshipers carry candles during the evening service to symbolize Christ's light in the world, after which a candlelit procession emerges from and reenters the church. Some Christians offer penance by fasting or abstaining from meat on this day.

Christmas is celebrated in the traditional manner with feasting, churchgoing, and an exchange of cards and gifts. The main shopping area is lit up and decorated, recordings of carols play continuously in the stores, and Santa makes his rounds in his traditional red costume in spite of the heat. The commercial emphasis on Christmas in Singapore allows it to be enjoyed with fervor by the entire community.

NONRELIGIOUS CELEBRATIONS

Singaporeans remember their country's beginnings as an independent nation each August. The highlight of the celebrations is the National Day Parade. The parade theme changes every year, but there are always colorfully decorated floats, bands, and dancers to lead the spectators in the festivities. Military displays and thematic celebrations emphasize the growth of the young nation and focus on the nation-building goals that lie ahead. Songs are composed for the occasion. In some years young Singaporeans are treated to a huge street party complete with disk jockeys, dance music, disco lights, and special effects.

Other annual events include Teachers' Day, when teachers receive recognition for their efforts during the year. On Children's Day and Youth Day, outings, exhibitions, and concerts are organized for students. Valentine's Day, Mother's Day, Father's Day, and New Year's Eve are also celebrated.

Spectators cheering during Singapore's National Day celebrations.

CALENDAR OF EVENTS

JANUARY	NEW YEAR'S DAY—The first day of the Christian year
JANUARY/ FEBRUARY	CHINESE NEW YEAR—The most important Chinese festival, also referred to as the Lunar New Year or Spring Festival
	CHINGAY PARADE—Annual procession down the main shopping area marking the close of Chinese New Year celebrations
	THAIPUSAM—Hindu ritual of penance with kavadi processions between two temples
FEBRUARY	VALENTINE'S DAY—A day for lovers as in the West
MARCH/APRIL	GOOD FRIDAY—Remembering the crucifixion of Christ
	EASTER—Christian celebration of Christ's resurrection with processions and church services
	QINGMING—Chinese festival, whose name means "Clear and Bright," during which family ancestors are honored by visits to their graves
	HARI RAYA PUASA—Sighting of the new moon and the end of the fasting month of Ramadan for Muslims*
MAY	LABOR DAY—Day of rest for all workers
	MOTHER'S DAY—Celebration for mothers
MAY/JUNE	VESAK DAY—Celebration of three stages in the life of Buddha: his birth, his enlightenment, and his death
JUNE/JULY	DRAGON BOAT FESTIVAL—Annual international race in decorated boats held in honor of the ancient poet Qu Yuan
	HARI RAYA HAJI—Muslim festival commemorating the annual pilgrimage of Muslims to the holy city of Mecca*
	YOUTH DAY—Concerts, exhibitions, and parade held in honor of the youth of Singapore
	FATHER'S DAY—Celebration of the father's role in society
AUGUST	MARKET FESTIVAL—Precursor to the Festival of the Hungry Ghosts when market stall-holders put on lavish feasts to ensure business will prosper in the coming year

	FESTIVAL OF THE HUNGRY GHOSTS—Chinese worship of souls released from purgatory
	NATIONAL DAY—Celebration of Singapore's independence
SEPTEMBER	LANTERN/MOONCAKE/MID-FALL FESTIVAL—Chinese celebration of the moon
	NAVRATRI—Hindu celebration in honor of the three consorts of the Hindu Trinity
OCTOBER/ NOVEMBER	CHILDREN'S DAY—For all those under 12 years of age
	THIMITHI—Fire-walking festival of Hindus to fulfill vows
	DEEPAVALI—Hindu festival celebrating the victory of good over evil
	MAULIDIN NABI—Birthday of the prophet Muhammad*
DECEMBER	CHRISTMAS—Christian celebration of the birth of Christ

Note that these dates follow the lunar calendar and are subject to change.

INTERNET LINKS

http://singaporefoodfestival.com.sg/

Singapore and its people are widely known for their food and their love of eating. It's no wonder then that the island would organize a food festival. Read more about it at this website.

www.singaporeartsfest.com/

As part of its promotion of the arts and culture, the organizers of the Singapore Arts Festival bring in top artists and performers.

www.singaporegardenfestival.com/

A festival for flora and garden enthusiasts!

FOOD

A man making *murtabak* in an Indian restaurant.

13

SINGAPORE IS UNIQUE IN SOUTHEAST Asia for its great variety of cuisines, the most interesting of which evolved from the traditions of early immigrants through settlement and intermarriage. While each culture kept up its traditional cooking, it could not help but absorb and modify food ideas from other immigrants with which it came in contact. To define the typical Singapore cuisine is therefore very difficult.

MAIN ETHNIC GROUPS AND THEIR CUISINES

THE CHINESE Although most Chinese migrants came to Singapore from southern China, they were a mixed people from a variety of provinces, each with its own distinctive cuisine. Their various cuisines were simple meals centered on rice, though some wheat-based dishes, such as steamed dumplings and noodles, came from northern China. The resulting assortment of dishes grew as people from different provinces borrowed ideas from one another.

Pork is a favorite with the Chinese, followed by poultry and fish. Lamb is considered too "heavy," while beef in large quantities is thought by some to be bad for the body. Fresh vegetables play an important role.

Singapore's cuisine is an important part of its culture and cultural identity. One of the nation's favorite pastimes is eating, and many blogs and television programs are devoted to food. Singaporean cuisine has been and is influenced by the different ethnic groups that live there. A huge variety of cuisines can be found there.

Chili crab is one of Singapore's most famous and beloved dishes.

Indeed, all the ingredients must be fresh, with only a little added seasoning, and amounts are balanced to provide both variety and texture.

THE MALAYS When Islam was introduced to the Malays in the 14th century, it was brought not by Arabs but by Indian Muslims from Gujarat in northwest India. From them, the Malays also inherited many Middle Eastern dishes with Indian influence.

Fish and chicken are eaten most often. Beef is enjoyed sometimes, mutton less often, and pork is forbidden to Muslims. Rice is the basis of a Malay meal, which usually includes vegetables with some fish, meat, or eggs, and *sambal* (sahm-bahl) accompaniments such as a chutney or sauce.

THE PERANAKANS This is perhaps the only cuisine that can be said to be truly Singaporean, springing from a unique blend of Malay and Chinese cultures and developed by the Straits Chinese. However, it is time-consuming to prepare and, because of this, quickly disappearing in modern Singapore.

Chinese ingredients are used but taste quite different when Malay ingredients are added. Interestingly, the Straits Chinese adopted Malay customs and rituals but not their religion, so pork is eaten. Their pork satay is similar to the Malay dish but sweeter. In addition, their cakes and sweets are much enjoyed by Singaporean Chinese whose own food traditions do not place much emphasis on desserts.

THE INDIANS The Tamils from the southeast Indian state of Tamil Nadu have always been a close-knit community, but foods brought to Singapore by Indian traders from Madras, Kerala, Sri Lanka, Pakistan, Punjab, and Persia have had long-term effects on their cuisine.

Though, strictly speaking, Hindus are vegetarians and do not consume meat, fish, or even eggs, many now eat mutton and chicken, though not

CHINESE	**CHICKEN RICE** *Small pieces of sliced chicken flavored with chilies, ginger, and soy sauce and served with rice cooked in chicken stock.*
	FRIED *KWAY TEOW* *Large flat rice noodles, fried with a mixture of prawns, pork, cockles, and bean sprouts.*
	DIM SUM *Lunchtime assortment of bite-size dumplings, rolls, and buns, stuffed with a variety of meats, prawns, and vegetables, served hot in bamboo trays.*
MALAY	**SATAY** *Small pieces of meat on skewers, grilled over a charcoal fire and served with a peanut sauce, small packets of rice wrapped in coconut leaves, and sliced cucumbers and onions.*
	NASI PADANG *Selection of meat, fish, and vegetable dishes, originally from Padang in West Sumatra. All are hot and spicy and served with plain rice.*
PERANAKAN	**CHILI CRAB** *Pieces of crab still in their shell, fried in a chili-and-soy-sauce paste.*
	POPIAH *A filling of shredded turnip, egg, prawns, garlic, and sprouts, spiced with sweet black and hot sauce, wrapped in a thin wheat flour pancake.*
	OTAK-OTAK *Fish mixed with pounded spices and coconut milk, wrapped in coconut leaves and grilled over a charcoal fire.*
INDIAN	**THOSAI** *Paper-thin, slightly sour pancake made of rice flour and lentils.*
	MURTABAK *Savory pancake filled with lightly seasoned minced mutton or chicken and onions, served with curry and cucumbers topped with ketchup.*
	FISH HEAD CURRY *Large fish head cooked in curry gravy.*

A spread of Peranakan food, a delicious and unique blend of both Chinese and Malay cuisine.

on Friday, which is a day of prayer. Some Hindus will not touch pork, not for religious reasons so much as because it is considered "unclean."

THE EURASIANS In Singapore, Eurasians are generally people of Portuguese and Indian or Sri Lankan descent whose food is a combination of East and West. Many dishes have their origins in Goa, which was a Portuguese area of India. Wine and sherry are added to their curries, and seasonings make their olive oil hot and spicy. Their cuisine, like that of the Peranakans, is slowly dying away as more Eurasians marry into the other Asian ethnic groups of Singapore.

FOODS AND THEIR SOURCES

Rice is an essential part of local meals, but as none is grown in Singapore, it is imported from abroad. Noodles are also a favorite, especially as a snack. These are available freshly made or as a packaged instant variety.

Meat, fish, poultry, and bean curd are the main sources of protein. A proportion of the chickens and ducks eaten are reared on special farms in the northwestern part of the island; the rest are imported. The rearing of pigs has been phased out due to limited land space. Beef and mutton are brought in from Australia, New Zealand, and elsewhere.

Fish are caught and brought to the auction markets in the early hours of the morning. Since Singaporeans eat a lot of fish and other seafood, much of it still has to be imported.

Most vegetable farms are in the northwest, where there is less urban development, but as Singapore's soil is not very fertile, hydroponic experiments are in progress to grow plants in nutrient-rich water without

VARIETIES OF LOCAL FRUIT

DURIAN This "king of fruits" is large and round with a tough skin covered with thick spikes. Inside, large seeds are enclosed in creamy flesh. Its notoriously strong and pungent smell is unpleasant to some but is considered delightful by local durian lovers.

MANGOSTEEN A thick, hard, purplish black skin encloses tiny segments of sweet, white flesh.

RAMBUTAN This is a small white-fleshed fruit enclosed in a bright red hairy skin. (Rambut means "hair" in Malay.)

PAPAYA A bright orange, oval fruit containing small black seeds, which are not eaten.

using soil. Nevertheless, more than half of all Singapore's vegetables come from Malaysia and other neighboring countries. Green and leafy vegetables are the main vegetables eaten, as well as tubers, water chestnuts, bamboo shoots, and bean sprouts.

Imported fresh fruit such as apples, oranges, pears, and grapes, as well as a great variety of tropical fruit, is available all year round in Singapore. Mangosteens, papayas, rambutans, and jackfruits are grown in the country, whereas mangoes, pineapples, and watermelons come from elsewhere in the region.

A great variety of canned, packaged, and preserved foods are prepared in factories in Singapore as well as imported from abroad. Ingredients for many cuisines are flown in daily.

KITCHENS

Kitchens tend to be very simply organized, and even fine meals are generally cooked with inexpensive, traditional utensils that continue to be favorites, along with the modern rice cooker and the microwave oven.

In a Singapore kitchen, a *kuali* (kwah-lee), or wok, is considered indispensable. This is a wide, bowllike pan with a curving base and high, sloping sides. It is usually made of heavy iron. Stir-frying, deep-frying, steaming, and boiling are the preferred ways of cooking.

In addition to the wok, a *batu lesong* (bah-too leh-sowng) is used. This is a hollowed-out granite bowl with a granite pestle for grinding seasonings such as onions, chilies, fresh turmeric, and garlic. Terra-cotta or clay pots are used in cooking because these are said to improve the taste of curries and are decorative as well as useful.

EATING HABITS

Rice is the basis of all meals and is accompanied by three to five other dishes and condiments. A Chinese meal will include soup, fish, something made with pork, and some vegetables. Each place setting will have a pair of chopsticks, a rice bowl, a small plate for the main course, and a tiny dish for sauces. In addition there will be a teacup or a glass for hot Chinese tea or iced water.

Hindu devotees at a temple having a meal. Eating using their hands is common practice with Indians and Malays alike.

Malay families serve a fish or meat dish, a vegetable dish, and a chili *sambal*, usually in common serving dishes. In today's urban environment people will sit at a Western table, using forks and spoons, but many still use their hands to eat. Knives are unnecessary, since the food is always in bite-sized pieces.

Indian meals follow a similar pattern to Malay ones, except for vegetarian meals that include a range of vegetable and lentil dishes instead of fish or meat. These are served with plain rice and a small serving of cool yogurt. Indian meals are sometimes served on square-cut banana leaves. A glass of cold water will be placed on the left, since the right hand is used for eating.

EATING OUT

Cuisines from around the world are available in Singapore. It is hard to believe such a tiny island can offer Indian, Chinese, Arab, Japanese, Thai, Korean, and Vietnamese food, as well as almost all types of Western food, from top European restaurants in major hotels to American fast-food outlets in shopping centers.

A Malay chef stirring a pot of chicken curry. Muslims adhere to strict religious regulation when it comes to food preparation and consumption.

Ordinary local "hawker" fare differs from home-cooked and restaurant food in its simplicity and speed of preparation. Traveling food sellers, or hawkers, once found this an easy way to earn a living. One-man mobile kitchens sold noodles, spring rolls, Indian breads with curry, fish porridge, and fruit juices. With the shift to a more urban lifestyle, they have been moved to permanent sites but continue to be known as hawkers, while the food centers where they sell their food are known as hawker centers.

Each hawker stall has a large advertising sign and may specialize in one or more types of food. All are licensed, and inspectors make regular checks to ensure high standards of sanitation.

Local food in hawker centers is inexpensive and popular, while eating out at hotels and restaurants is comparatively expensive. Singaporeans can happily lunch in a foreign restaurant, snack at a hawker center, and then return to their own ethnic group's home cooking.

FOOD TABOOS

Muslims can eat only food that is halal—that is, conforms to their religious restrictions. Eating pork is forbidden, as is drinking alcohol and eating meat that has not been slaughtered by another Muslim. Neither Muslims nor Indians eat with the left hand, although they do pass food around with this hand and use it to hold a glass.

Hindus are forbidden to eat beef because the cow is considered a sacred animal. Many Hindus are vegetarian, because they believe they will experience a similar pain if they take the life of a living thing unnecessarily. These strict Hindus and Buddhists do not eat eggs either, because they are an animal product.

CHOPSTICKS

The first chopsticks of ancient China were probably twigs or bamboo sticks used to prevent fingers from getting burned. Since then, chopsticks have been made of wood, bone, ivory, jade, and silver. The emperors of China believed that if their food was poisoned, their silver chopsticks would become discolored.

Today many Chinese families in Singapore use forks and spoons and use chopsticks only for certain dishes. Children begin using chopsticks at around four years of age for any food that is easy to pick up. They soon learn that food can also be pressed, pulled, and broken with them.

There is a chopstick etiquette to be learned, too. It is rude to wave chopsticks while eating or to leave them stuck in a bowl of rice. They should not rest on the rice bowl; this is a sign that there was not enough food.

In Singapore, it is not unusual to see non-Chinese using chopsticks with ease.

FOOD BELIEFS

The Chinese and the Indians believe the type of food eaten creates a certain kind of person and that eating should be for both body and spirit. They also believe that gods eat, too, and they offer food to the deities as a sign of respect and thanksgiving and a way to ensure future blessings, especially during festive occasions or the gods' birthdays. Eating the food offered is a symbol of their communication with the god.

Most Singaporeans believe that food is "heaty" (full of heat) or "cooling," depending on its effect on the body. Examples of "heaty" foods are chocolate, fried foods, and meat. These make the body feel too hot, full, and uncomfortable. To counteract the upset these foods cause, cooling foods such as tomatoes, cucumbers, watermelons, or herbal soups are prescribed to restore "inner" balance. Illness can be caused by eating heaty foods, but cooling foods can also cause or aggravate colds and should not be eaten on cool days.

TABLE MANNERS

The normal practice when serving food in homes is to place all the dishes in the center of the table at the beginning of the meal so that people can help themselves as the meal progresses. It is important to take only what is needed because it is considered impolite to waste food.

In Chinese restaurants, there are usually 10 courses in a meal, and one course is presented at a time. The Chinese like to eat as a communal group with an even number of diners, whereas in more conservative Malay and Indian homes, the men eat first, followed by the women. This traditional, discriminating practice is not as common today, though, as in the past.

Both Malays and Indians eat with the fingers of the right hand. The Malays scoop up a little food in the hollow of their bent fingers, never soiling the palm of their hand. Unlike the Malays, the Indians press and roll their food into a small ball using their fingers and palms and then carry it to the mouth with the fingertips. Sucking or licking the fingers is considered bad manners.

FEASTS

Chinese feasts can stretch to 12 courses: The more festive the occasion, the more courses that are offered. As the number of guests at celebrations such as weddings or birthdays can be large, and the meal does not begin until all the guests have arrived, Chinese dinners have a tendency to start late. Today hosts try to encourage their guests to be punctual.

There is an art in selecting courses. They are chosen to harmonize with each other in taste, color, and texture. The first course is usually a cold appetizer, followed by some dry dishes, and then some with sauce. Spicy dishes are set against more-subtle ones and the soft against the crispy. Filling soups, fried rice, or noodles are traditionally served during the second-to-last course, to ensure no guest goes home hungry.

A Malay feast is generally a dinner party held at home, a thanksgiving *kenduri*, or a wedding. Guests arrive on time or earlier and will even help with the preparations. *Nasi minyak* (nah-see mee-yah)—rice prepared with ghee, milk or yogurt, onions, and garlic—is commonly served at Malay weddings to symbolize prosperity. By tradition, guests at Malay weddings also receive wrapped and decorated eggs, symbols of fertility.

Muslims keep treats for the end of the fasting month, such as tarts filled with fresh pineapple jam or peanut biscuits. A range of foreign-influenced dishes are always served—*rendang daging* (rehn-dahng dah-gehng), a Sumatran dish of beef in coconut milk; *ayam korma* (ah-yahm core-mah), a chicken dish of Middle Eastern origin; and Javanese *tempe* (tam-pay), fermented soybean cake fried with fresh prawns and peanuts.

At Hindu wedding celebrations, people arrive on time and leave about a half-hour after the feast. Vegetarian food is set out on long tables. Sour rice must never be served at Hindu weddings, and the dishes must not be too hot, too spicy, or salty, because this spells bad luck for the newlyweds.

Northern Indian meals are strictly vegetarian during Deepavali, whereas southern Indians serve a variety of meat dishes. Favorite festival foods are *muruku* (moo-roo-koo), a savory chip of rice flour and spices; ghee balls, a mixture of ghee, ground green beans, brown sugar, and cashew nuts; and *kesari* (kay-sah-ree), made of semolina, ghee, cashew nuts, and raisins.

INTERNET LINKS

http://ieatishootipost.sg/

One of Singapore's most popular food blogs, which provides information about the quality of food and even a little food history!

www.makansutra.com/index.php

Singapore's go-to food guide with videos and pictures that covers just about everything that Singaporeans eat.

www.makantime.com/indexrecipes.html

A comprehensive list of Singaporean recipes.

CHA SHAO (ROAST PORK)

This is a popular lunchtime meal. It can be eaten with a plate of noodles or rice, accompanied by slices of cucumber and tomato.

Ingredients

1 pound (500 g) pork (a cut with some fat on it is best, like the shoulder)

2 teaspoons (10 ml) honey or sugar

1 tablespoon (15 ml) dark soy sauce

1 tablespoon (15 ml) light soy sauce

a few drops of red food coloring

Sauce

2 cups (475 ml) pork stock or water

1 tablespoon cornstarch

a pinch of Chinese five-spice powder

Slice the pork into strips, about 1 inch (2.5 cm) thick and 1 inch (2.5 cm) wide. Mix the rest of the ingredients, and marinate the meat for at least two hours. Grill the pork over medium heat on all sides until done, basting the meat often with the rest of the marinade. This should take about a half-hour. The sugar in the marinade will cause some caramelizing on areas that are closer to the heat, giving the pork its characteristic burnt look. Allow the meat to cool to the touch. Then cut it into slices and serve on plain boiled noodles or steamed white rice, garnished with tomato and cucumber slices.

For the sauce, collect the drippings from the roast pork. Add pork stock or water, cornstarch, and Chinese five-spice powder. Mix it together in a saucepan and bring it to a boil until it thickens. Pour the sauce over the roast pork and noodles or rice.

SAGO PUDDING WITH PALM SUGAR

This is a sweet dessert pudding that uses a special kind of palm sugar, called *gula melaka* in Malay. The sugar can be bought in grocery stores selling Asian foods.

Ingredients

1 cup (250 ml) pearl sago or tapioca seeds

2 cups (475 ml) water

1 cup (237 ml) coconut milk

pinch of salt

½ ounce (200 g) palm sugar (use dark brown sugar as a substitute if palm sugar is not available)

Wash the sago and soak in water for a few minutes. Put the sago and water over heat, and simmer gently until the sago appears translucent and the mixture is clear and thick. Add coconut milk and a pinch of salt, stirring constantly until the mixture is very thick. Turn it into a mold and chill in the refrigerator until it is set. When ready to eat, melt the palm sugar over low heat with a little water if necessary.

To serve, turn out the molded pudding into individual cups. Top with the liquid sugar and more coconut milk. You may also add small cubes of fruits in the dessert.

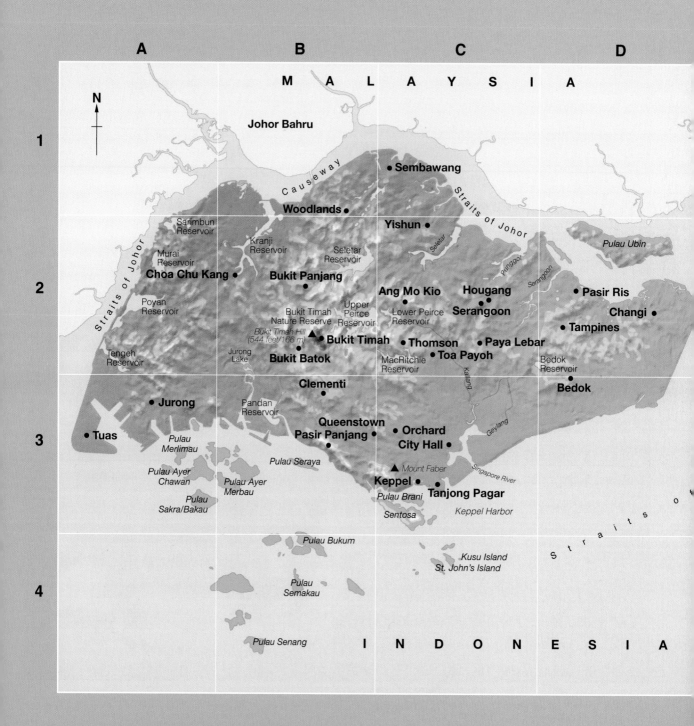

MAP OF SINGAPORE

Ang Mo Kio, C2

Bedok, D2—D3
Bedok Reservoir, C2—D2
Bukit Batok, B2
Bukit Panjang, B2
Bukit Timah, B2
Bukit Timah Hill, B2
Bukit Timah Nature Reserve, B2

Causeway, B1
Changi, D2
Choa Chu Kang, B2
City Hall, C3
Clementi, B3

Geylang River, C3

Hougang, C2

Indonesia, B4—D4

Johor Bahru, B1
Jurong, A3
Jurong Lake, B2

Kallang River, C2—C3
Keppel, C3
Keppel Harbor, C3
Kranji Reservoir, B2
Kusu Island, C4

Lower Peirce Reservoir, C2

MacRitchie Reservoir, C2

Malaysia, A1—D1, A2, E1—2
Mount Faber, C3
Murai Reservoir, A2

Orchard, C3

Pandan Reservoir, B3
Pasir Panjang, B3
Pasir Ris, D2
Paya Lebar, C2
Poyan Reservoir, A2
Pulau Ayer Chawan, A3
Pulau Ayer Merbau, B3
Pulau Brani, C3
Pulau Bukum, B3—B4
Pulau Merlimau, A3
Pulau Sakra/Bakau, A3
Pulau Semakau, B4
Pulau Senang, B4
Pulau Seraya, B3
Pulau Tekong, E1—E2
Pulau Tekong Reservoir, E2
Pulau Ubin, D2
Punggol River, C2

Queenstown, B3

Saint John's Island, C4
Sarimbun Reservoir, A2
Seletar Reservoir, B2
Seletar River, C2
Sembawang, C1
Sentosa, C3
Serangoon, C2
Serangoon River, D2—C2
Singapore River, C3
Straits of Johor, A1—2, B1, C1—C2
Straits of Singapore, D3—4, E3

Tampines, D2
Tengeh Reservoir, A2
Thomson, C2
Toa Payoh, C2
Tuas, A3

Upper Peirce Reservoir, B2

Woodlands, B1

Yishun, C2

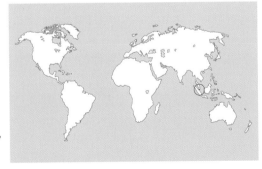

ECONOMIC SINGAPORE

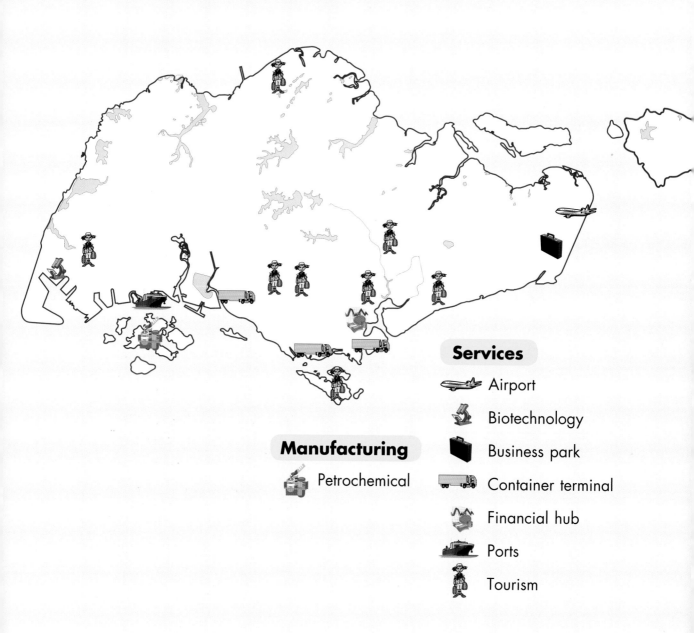

Manufacturing

Petrochemical

Services

Airport

Biotechnology

Business park

Container terminal

Financial hub

Ports

Tourism

ABOUT THE ECONOMY

OVERVIEW

Singapore has one of the highest per capita GDPs in the world. This highly successful and wealthy economy is a capitalist free-market economy with some governmental control. The economy is competitive, open, and well known for being corruption-free. Singapore is reliant on international trade and promotes this by its excellent infrastructure. The country is trying to diversify its economy by developing its services sector, as well as its biotechnology, chemical, and petrochemical industries.As its economy is heavily orientated toward exports, Singapore was hurt by the global economic crisis of 2007—10. With help from the government's "resilience package," amounting to $15 billion, the economy recovered slightly in the later quarters of 2009. In the 2010 budget, the government announced a long-term target of 3—5 percent growth over the next decade.

WORKFORCE

3.03 million

UNEMPLOYMENT RATE

3 percent (2009)

CURRENCY

US$1 = S$1.23 (June 2011)
$1 = 100 cents

GROSS DOMESTIC PRODUCT (GDP)

$182.2 billion (2009 est.)

INFLATION RATE

0.6 percent (2009)

AIRPORT

Eight airports with paved runways

SHIPPING

One of the world's top bunkering ports. Also one of the world's busiest ports in terms of shipping tonnage in 2009. The total tonnage of ships was 45.6 million gross tons (46.3 million metric tons) in 2009.

ROADWAYS

2,085 miles (3,356 km)

MAJOR INDUSTRIES

Electronics, chemicals, financial services, oil-drilling equipment, petroleum refining, rubber processing and rubber products, processed food and beverages, ship repair, offshore platform construction, life sciences, entrepôt trade

MAJOR IMPORTS (2009)

Machinery and equipment, mineral fuels, chemicals, foodstuffs, consumer goods

MAJOR EXPORTS (2009)

Machinery and equipment (including electronics), consumer goods, pharmaceuticals and other chemicals, mineral fuels

CULTURAL SINGAPORE

Sri Mariamman Temple
The famous Sri Mariamman Indian Temple on South Bridge Road was built in 1823 by Indian pioneer Naraina Pillai, a government clerk who had followed Raffles from Penang in 1819. This typical southern Indian temple, topped by a pagoda-shaped tower at its main entrance, is dedicated to the goddess Mariamman.

Singapore Zoological Gardens
Set on a 69-acre (28-hectare) site in a green reservoir belt, it houses more than 2,800 animals of over 200 species.

Night Safari
Part of the Singapore Zoo. A 99-acre (40-hectare) densely forested wildlife park that is open to visitors at night. Visitors can see more than 1,000 nocturnal animals, some roaming freely.

The National Museum of Singapore
Built in 1887, the National Museum is Singapore's oldest museum. It is home to 11 National Treasures: the Singapore Stone; the Gold Ornaments of the Sacred Hill from East Java; a daguerreotype of Singapore Town believed to be one of the earliest photographs of Singapore; the will of writer Munshi Abdullah; the portrait of colonial official Sir Frank Swettenham; the hearse of businessman and activist Tan Jiak Kim; a Peranakan coffin cover; the mace of the City of Singapore commemorating King George VI's raising of the island's status to a city in 1951; the elaborate 1930s Xin Sai Le puppet stage; early settler William Farquhar's drawings of flora and fauna; and a portrait of former Singapore governor Sir Shenton Thomas.

Little India
Shophouses and stalls selling Indian textiles, flower garlands, spices, and cuisine.

Singapore River
Once the lifeline of Singapore, this was a busy route plied by bumboats ferrying cargo between ships anchored in the harbor and warehouses on the riverbanks. The warehouses have been converted into restaurants.

Esplanade Theatres on the Bay
The Esplanade was opened in 2002, and was slated to be Singapore's premier location for the Arts. It covers 15 acres (6 hectares) of land and is located near the mouth of the Singapore River.

Singapore Flyer
The Singapore Flyer is the world's largest observation wheel. It stands at 541 feet (165 m) above the ground and showcases panoramic views of Singapore.

Marina Bay Sands
The Marina Bay Sands is an integrated resort developed by Las Vegas Sands. It is home to one of Singapore's two casinos, and boasts luxury shopping, entertainment, theaters, the ArtScience Museum, and a SkyPark, which stands at 627 feet (191 m) above ground, perched atop the Marina Bay Sands.

Chinatown
A part of old Singapore now restored but still retaining its charm and character. Two-story buildings house shops selling Chinese medicinal herbs, gold jewelry, handicrafts, and souvenirs.

The Singapore Botanical Gardens
Sir Stamford Raffles, the founder of Singapore and a keen naturalist, established the first botanical and experimental garden on Government Hill (also known as Fort Canning Hill) in 1822, shortly after his arrival in Singapore. Today the 156-acre (63-ha) gardens consists of three "cores": Tanglin is the heritage core, retaining the old favorites and charms of the historic gardens; Central is the tourist belt; and Bukit Timah is the educational and recreational zone.

Sentosa
A nearby island where Singaporeans can enjoy the sun, sand, and sea. The many attractions include the Butterfly Park and Fort Siloso, a 19th-century fort. It is also home to the integrated resort, Resorts World Sentosa, which encompasses a casino, fine dining, and also Asia's first Universal Studios theme park.

The Merlion Statue (Merlion Park)
The Merlion is the symbol of Singapore. This is an imaginary creature with the head of a lion and the body of a fish. The lion head represents Singapore's original name, Singapura, meaning "lion city." There are five recognized Merlion statues in the country. In 2011, a functional temporary luxury hotel room was designed and built around the Merlion by artist Tatzu Nishi, as part of the Singapore Biennial.

OFFICIAL NAME
Republic of Singapore

CAPITAL
Singapore

DESCRIPTION OF FLAG
Two horizontal stripes, red above white. The red stripe represents equality and brotherhood; the white stripe, purity and virtue. On the hoist side of the flag is a white crescent moon and five stars representing democracy, peace, progress, justice, and equality.

NATIONAL ANTHEM
Majulah Singapura (Onward Singapore)

POPULATION
5,076,700 million (2010)

ETHNIC GROUPS
Malays: 13.4 percent, Chinese: 74.1 percent, Indians: 9.2 percent, others: 3.3 percent. (2010 estimate)

LIFE EXPECTANCY
82 years

LITERACY RATE
92.5 percent

LEADERS IN SPORTS
Gao Ning, 2009 SEA Games gold medalist, table tennis player; Feng Tianwei, 2008 Olympic silver medalist, table tennis player

LEADERS IN ART
Chong Soo Pieng, painter; Chen Wen Hsi, painter; Liu Kang, painter; Brother Joseph McNally, sculptor

SYSTEM OF GOVERNMENT
Parliamentary democracy. Elected president is head of state. Prime minister leads cabinet of ministers in the administration of the government. All ministers are appointed from elected members of parliament.

SOCIAL SECURITY
The Central Provident Fund is a comprehensive social-security savings plan to which all employers and workers must contribute. The fund may be used to pay for home ownership, medical care, and retirement expenses.

TIME LINE

IN SINGAPORE	IN THE WORLD
	1206–1368 Genghis Khan unifies the Mongols and starts conquest of the world. At its height, the Mongol Empire under Kublai Khan stretches from China to Persia and parts of Europe and Russia.
1300s Singapura, the "Lion City," is settled.	
	1776 U.S. Declaration of Independence
1819 Stamford Raffles founds Singapore.	**1789–99** The French Revolution
1826 Singapore, Penang, and Malacca become the Straits Settlements.	
1867 The Straits Settlements becomes a British crown colony.	
Late 1800s Singapore becomes a major port of call for ships plying between Europe and Asia.	
1914 British Malaya is formed out of the Straits Settlements and the Malay States.	**1914** World War I begins.
	1939 World War II begins.
1942 The Japanese occupy Singapore.	
1945 Singapore returns to British rule.	**1945** The United States drops atomic bombs on Hiroshima and Nagasaki. World War II ends.
1946 Singapore becomes a crown colony.	
1948–60 Rise of communism results in a state of emergency being declared.	
1955 Singapore gains partial self-government. David Marshall becomes the first chief minister.	
1958 Singapore attains self-government. Lee Kuan Yew becomes the first prime minister.	
1963 Singapore becomes part of Malaysia.	

IN SINGAPORE	IN THE WORLD
1965 Singapore separates from Malaysia.	
1967 Singapore becomes part of ASEAN, the Association of Southeast Asian Nations.	
1990 Goh Chok Tong becomes prime minister.	
1998 Singapore enters recession for the first time in 13 years during Asian financial crisis.	**1997** Hong Kong is returned to China.
1999 Sellapan Ramanathan becomes president without election.	**2001** Terrorists crash planes into New York, Washington D.C., and Pennsylvania.
2003 Critical outbreak of SARS virus. Singapore becomes first Asian nation to sign free-trade deal with United States.	**2003** War in Iraq begins.
2004 Lee Hsien Loong becomes prime minister.	**2004** Eleven Asia countries hit by giant tsunami, killing at least 225,000 people.
2005 Government legalizes casino gambling.	**2005** Hurricane Katrina devastates the Gulf Coast of the United States.
2006 Lee Hsien Loong's ruling PAP wins general elections.	**2008** Earthquake in Sichuan, China, kills 67,000 people.
2009 Singapore recovers from its worst recession on record with economic growth of 20.4 percent between April and June.	**2009** Outbreak of flu virus H1N1 around the world
2010 Singapore hosts the inaugural Youth Olympics.	**2011** Twin earthquake and tsunami disasters strike northeast Japan, leaving over 14,000 dead and thousands more missing.

GLOSSARY

Coffee shops/hawker centers/food centers
Places selling good and reasonably priced food, these can be found everywhere.

halal
Muslims eat only food that is halal, or "allowed." This is food that has been specially prepared and is free from pork, a forbidden meat to Muslims.

hawkers
Once itinerant sellers of food, today all hawkers are found in food centers. This makes it possible for the government to license them and to conduct health checks.

HDB flats
Affordable public housing provided by the Housing and Development Bureau.

hongbao (hong-pao)
A red packet containing money, given as a gift on birthdays, weddings, and Chinese New Year.

kiasu (kee-ya-soo)
From the Hokkien dialect meaning "afraid to lose." An attitude of not wanting to lose out that Singaporeans think, in a tongue-in-cheek sort of way, characterizes them.

National Service
Mandatory three years of service in the armed forces required of all Singaporean males when they finish school and reach the age of 18.

Peranakan
Chinese who speak Baba Malay, a mixture of Malay and a Chinese dialect, Hokkien.

satay
Meat on wooden skewers, barbecued over hot coals and eaten with a peanut sauce.

Singlish
English spoken with a Singapore flavor, often incorporating Chinese and Malay words.

FOR FURTHER INFORMATION

BOOKS

Bravo-Bhasin, Marion. *Singapore: a Survival Guide to Customs and Etiquette (Culture Shock)*. London: Marshall Cavendish Corporation, 2009.

Davidson, G.W.H., and Yeap Chin Aik. *A Naturalist's Guide to the Birds of Malaysia and Singapore*. Oxford, England: John Beaufoy Publishing Ltd, 2010.

Discovery Channel. *The History of Singapore: Lion City, Asian Tiger*. Hoboken, NJ: John Wiley, 2010.

Eveland, Jennifer. *DK Eyewitness Top 10 Travel Guide: Singapore*. London: Dorling Kindersley, 2009.

Lewis, Mark Quartet. *The Rough Guide to Singapore*. London: Rough Guides, 2010.

Oakley, Matt. *Singapore: City Guide*. London: Lonely Planet Publications, 2009.

Singapore Complete Residents' Guide. Singapore: Explorer Publishing , 2007.

Singapore Insight Step by Step Guide. Singapore: APA Publications Pte. Ltd., 2009.

Tan, Terry, and Christopher Tan. *Singapore Cooking: Fabulous Recipes from Asia's Food Capital*. North Clarendon, VT: Tuttle Publishing, 2009.

Time Out Singapore. 1st ed. London: Time Out Guides Ltd., 2007.

Turnbull, C. M. *A History of Modern Singapore, 1819-2005*. Singapore: Singapore University Press, 2009.

WEBSITES

CIA World Factbook: Singapore. www.cia.gov/library/publications/the-world-factbook/geos/sn.html

Singapore Government. www.gov.sg/government/web/content/govsg/classic/home

Singapore Tourism Board. www.stb.gov.sg/

ThinkQuest: Evolution of Singapore. http://library.thinkquest.org/12405/developing.htm

FILMS/DVDS

History of Singapore. Discovery Channel, 2008

Panorama Singapore. TravelVideoStore.com, 2005.

Tanamera—Lion of Singapore. Simply Media, 1989.

BIBLIOGRAPHY

BOOKS

Hoe, Irene. *Singapore*. New York: Passport Books, 1989.

Houghton, Graham, and Julia Wakefield. *Singapore*. South Melbourne, Australia: Macmillan, 1986.

Insight Guide. *Singapore*. Boston: Houghton Mifflin, 1994.

Lloyd, Ian, and Betty Schafer. *Singapore*. Singapore: Times Editions, 1989.

WEBSITES

ClimateTemp: Singapore. www.climatetemp.info/singapore/

Economy Watch: Singapore Economy. www.economywatch.com/world_economy/singapore/

Energy Market Authority: Singapore Gas Industry. www.ema.gov.sg/page/114/id:48/

Maps of World: Singapore. www.mapsofworld.com/singapore/singapore-location-map.html

Migration Information Source—Singapore. www.migrationinformation.org/Profiles/display.cfm?ID=570

MPA Singapore: Singapore's 2009 Maritime Performance. www.mpa.gov.sg/sites/global_navigation/news_center/mpa_news/mpa_news_detail.page?filename=nr100107.xml

Singapore Cabinet Government. www.cabinet.gov.sg/index.htm

Singapore Government. www.gov.sg/

Singapore National Youth Council Website. www.nyc.pa.gov.sg/

ThinkQuest: Land Reclamation in Singapore. http://library.thinkquest.org/C006891/reclamation.html

INDEX

architecture, 6, 99
area (land), 12, 14, 21, 24, 45, 47, 55, 59, 83, 114, 116, 122
army, 25, 72
   National Service, 6, 72, 77
arts
   bangsawan, 94
   calligraphy, 83, 99
   dance, 92, 94, 95—96, 98, 105, 112, 115
   drama, 94, 95, 96
   dragon dance, 92
   handicrafts, 97
   music, 94, 95, 96—97, 98, 110, 112, 115
   paintings, 97
   pottery, 41, 99
   puppet shows, 93
   sculptures, 97
   singing, 58, 96, 101, 107
   textiles, 97

beliefs, 71, 77, 79, 80, 84—85, 88
birds, 16, 47, 107, 110
birth, 68, 70, 71, 84, 110, 116, 117
   birthrate, 63, 66, 69
buildings, 45, 49, 81, 82, 84

cabinet, 22, 27, 28, 29, 33
celebrations, 72, 74, 115, 116, 128, 129
   National Day Parade, 115
ceremonies, 71, 75
children, 9, 32, 58, 59, 63, 65, 66, 67, 68, 69, 70, 75, 82, 102, 106, 110, 111, 115, 127
China, 5, 6, 12, 19, 24, 42, 43, 47, 54, 81, 85, 90, 94, 102, 105, 109, 110, 119, 127
citizens, 5, 6, 21, 28, 30, 58, 64, 65, 72, 91
classes, 8, 24, 80, 93, 95
climate, 9, 11, 14—15, 17, 47
clothes, 39, 41, 60, 76, 110, 111
colonial rule
   British, 7, 8, 19, 20, 21, 22, 23, 25, 27, 30, 54, 89, 90, 104
   Dutch, 21, 53, 90

Japanese, 7, 22, 23, 24, 25, 38, 65, 99, 106, 125
   Portuguese, 7, 20, 57, 122
communications, 8, 23, 58, 127
   roads, 14, 23, 45, 48, 54
community centers, 31, 95, 103, 106, 107
Confucianism, 27, 63, 81
construction, 39, 43
cooking, 119, 124, 126
cuisine, 9, 59, 119, 120, 122, 123
customs, 24, 57, 58, 59, 61, 71, 79, 81, 120

death, 24, 33, 76—77, 81, 85, 109, 110, 116
democracy, 6, 22

eating, 9, 106, 125, 126, 127
   hawker centers, 9, 51, 126
   restaurants, 9, 14, 73, 98, 102, 125, 126, 128
education, 8, 23, 38, 42, 47, 66, 67, 68, 75, 81
   schools, 8, 9 , 31, 58, 66, 67, 69, 73, 91, 97, 103
elderly, 84, 104, 107
elections, 6, 27, 29, 30, 32
entertainment, 42, 96, 104
ethnicity, 21, 58
exports, 35, 41

factories, 13, 31, 123
family, 9, 17, 24, 32, 41, 42, 57, 58, 59, 62, 63, 64, 65, 66, 67, 69, 70, 71, 74, 75, 77, 88, 106, 109, 110, 114, 116, 124, 125, 127
feasts, 71, 75, 116, 128, 129
festivals
   Christmas, 114
   Deepavali, 113, 114, 129
   Dragon Boat Festival, 109
   Good Friday, 114
   Hari Raya Haji, 112
   Hari Raya Puasa, 111
   Hungry Ghosts, 110, 116
   Lunar New Year, 110, 116, 124

   Mid-Autumn, 110
   Navratri, 112
   Qingming, 109
   Thaipusam, 112, 113
   Thimithi, 113
   Vesak Day, 110
fishing, 5, 56, 101, 104
foreign workers, 5, 43
forests, 12, 47
fruits, 98, 110, 123, 126

games, 102—103
gardens, 11, 12, 14, 46, 47, 48

harbors, 5, 12, 36
health, 8, 24, 46, 49, 51, 64
   hygiene, 51
   medicine, 22, 84
heritage, 24, 93, 97, 101
hobbies, 101—102, 106, 107
Hong Kong, 6, 35, 38, 42
housing, 6, 14, 23, 24, 31, 54, 64, 65, 67, 74, 83, 107
   condominiums, 8, 65
   Housing and Development Board (HDB), 24, 31, 65

immigrants, 24, 36, 54, 55, 57, 79, 119
independence, 7, 9, 22—23, 58, 68, 117
India, 5, 21, 27, 42, 43, 52, 54, 57, 63, 78, 81, 87, 90, 96, 113, 120, 122
Indonesia, 38, 42, 43, 49, 50, 53, 56, 67, 90
industries, 38, 40, 48
infrastructure, 8, 23, 39
insects, 17, 51
islets, 11, 12, 101
   Pulau Tekong, 11, 72
   Pulau Ubin, 11, 47, 48
   Sentosa, 11, 12, 42, 105

jewelry, 61
justice, 33, 58
   courts, 9, 33, 106

kitchens, 123—124, 126

INDEX

lakes, 13, 101
languages, 7, 58, 87, 89, 90, 98
    dialects, 8, 24, 87, 88, 91
    English, 8, 23, 35, 58, 59, 81, 87,
      88, 89, 90, 91, 93, 94
    Mandarin, 87, 91
    Singlish, 8, 87, 88, 89, 91
    Tamil, 59, 87, 90, 120
laws, 27, 48
Lee Kuan Yew, 23, 27, 29, 32, 33
libraries, 31, 98, 105
literacy, 87, 98
literature, 80, 90, 98, 105

manufacturing, 37, 38, 39
maps
    Cultural Singapore, 136
    Economic Singapore, 134
    Map of Singapore, 133
markets, 31, 37, 42, 111, 122
marriage, 61, 74, 75, 76, 110, 114
    divorce, 66, 76
    intermarriage, 57, 119
    weddings, 61, 74, 75, 96, 128, 129
meals, 9, 119, 122, 123, 124, 125, 129
meats, 114, 120, 121, 125—127, 129, 130
media, 30, 73
    magazines, 30
    newspapers, 30
    radio, 41, 80, 91
    television, 41, 69, 91, 105, 106, 119
men, 20, 25, 55, 72, 73, 76, 77, 80,
    82, 87, 88, 94, 100, 105, 107, 128
military, 65, 72, 103
monsoons, 11, 15
multiculturalism, 58, 61, 89

names, 58, 59
natural resources, 7, 9, 23, 32, 36, 37
nature reserves, 12, 16, 47—48

parks, 11, 12, 14, 39, 45, 46, 48, 75,
    101, 103
parliament, 26, 28
pastimes, 9, 106, 119
people
    Arabs, 55, 120

Chinese, 53—56, 58—61
    Cantonese, 54, 85, 87, 96
    Hakkas, 54
    Hokkiens, 54
    Teochews, 54
Eurasians, 53, 55, 57, 61, 122
Europeans, 55
Indians, 52, 54, 55, 57—58, 60, 61
    Bengalis, 57
    Gujaratis, 57
    Punjabis, 57
    Tamils, 57, 120
Malays, 56—61
    Boyanese, 56
    Bugis, 53, 56
    Orang Laut, 20, 56
    Peranakans, 59, 122
permanent residency (PR), 6, 21
plants, 16, 40, 47, 50, 122
political parties, 22, 25, 27, 29, 30, 31
pollution, 48
population, 5, 6, 7, 8, 10, 11, 13, 21,
    23, 24, 36, 45, 46, 54, 55, 57, 59,
    65, 79, 87, 96
ports, 5, 19, 21, 23, 34, 41
prime minister, 22, 27, 28, 29, 32, 33

races, 23, 30, 42, 58, 64, 75, 79,
    109, 116
rainfall, 13, 15
rain forests, 12, 16, 47
reading, 68, 86, 98
recipes
    Cha Shao (roast pork), 130
    Sago pudding with plum sugar,
    131
reclamation, 16, 45, 50, 102
recreation, 48, 101
religions
    Buddhism, 79, 80, 81
    Christianity, 81, 82
    Hinduism, 81
    Islam, 56, 80, 81, 120
    Taoism, 79, 81, 85
reservoirs, 13, 50, 101
residents' committees, 31, 64
rites, 71, 74

rituals, 71, 72, 75, 77, 82, 120
rivers, 12—13, 103, 104
    Singapore River, 12, 13, 20, 54,
    55, 62, 98

seasons, 11, 15
shopping, 9, 31, 42, 73, 89, 98, 106,
    107, 111, 114, 116, 125
soil, 77, 122, 123
Southeast Asia, 5, 7, 22, 32, 38, 80,
    81, 105, 119
sports, 9, 48, 101, 102, 103—104, 107
Stamford Raffles, 12, 18, 19, 20, 21,
    23, 24, 27, 32, 45, 55, 88
storytelling, 104—105, 107
Straits Settlements, 21—22
swamps, 12, 47
symbols, 71, 82, 90, 102, 129

technology, 35, 38, 39, 45, 50
temples, 6, 54, 80, 81, 82, 83, 112, 116
theaters, 93, 94, 98
topography, 12
tourism, 40
trading, 12, 19—24, 36, 37, 53
traffic, 13, 14, 41, 48, 101
transportation, 8, 38
    airport, 23
    Mass Rapid Transit (MRT), 8, 14
    railway, 22
    ships, 12, 19, 21, 22, 42
travel, 14, 105
trees, 14, 47, 48

unemployment, 22
United States, 41, 59, 105

values, 30, 58, 63, 66, 73, 88, 105
vegetables, 119, 120, 121, 123, 124

water, 13, 16, 45, 49, 50, 65, 109, 122,
    123, 124, 125, 130, 131
wildlife, 16, 47
women, 21, 55, 59, 60, 65, 67, 68—69,
    70, 73, 76, 77, 82, 87, 88, 113, 128
workforce, 35, 36, 37, 43, 67, 68, 69
World War II, 7, 22, 25, 64